Managing in Asia

What Readers Are Saying...

Drawing on his long experience doing business in Asia, Azar offers a compelling analysis of what it takes to succeed in business in Asia. His key insight, and one he illustrates with many important examples, is that what sets management in Asia apart from the West is not in what managers do but how they do it. Business executives who aim to succeed in Asian countries that are more and more at the center of the world economy would do well to read Azar's latest book.

Prof. Gerald Curtis
Burgess Professor Emeritus of Japanese Government
Columbia University

Robert Azar has amazingly keen insight, a truly valuable perspective and an extraordinary knowledge base on global dynamics. In this timely new scholarly endeavor, Azar offers us a wide array of thoughtful explanations and utilitarian recommendations on how to navigate the complex waters of international economic development with the cross-cultural competence so essential to producing positive outcomes. A must read.

Thomas J. White
Director
Economic Development Partnership
North Carolina State University
Former Director
North Carolina Department of Commerce

My IBM and Lenovo Marketing and Procurement career spanned thirty-seven years. Negotiation strategy and international negotiation were a key part of my responsibility and I learned through experience. I wish I had known Robert and had the opportunity to read his books early on in my career. His material is spot on and is invaluable to any business.

David Raymond
Former Marketing and Procurement Manager
IBM and Lenovo

I have known Robert Azar for a number of years. I find him to be a well-studied executive with a significant number of years of management experience. His views are certainly worth considering when engaging in business in Asian markets.

Santo J. Costa
Retired Vice Chairman and President
Quintiles Transnational Corporation

Having experienced business transactions in China, India, Japan, and Vietnam, I found Azar's book a clear and thorough presentation on doing business in Asia—a true *tour de force*. Azar is a forty-year experienced, in-the-trenches, business veteran who keenly understands Asian management styles. He provides the reader with enlightening guidance on the cultural values and social norms that form the foundation of each nation's management practices preparing the reader to better navigate doing business and building lasting relationships. A must read if you do business in Asia.

John L. Atkins, III
Honorary Counsel General of Japan in Raleigh NC 2009–2014

It has been my privilege over the past three decades to work on various projects with Robert Azar. Robert is unique among consultants because of his ability to combine his impressive book smarts with on-the-ground, practical advice. I'm glad to see that this book—his third on various aspects of doing business in Asia—continues in this vein. I am not aware of any other books that succeed as well in this regard. I strongly recommend them to anyone looking for practical help with doing business in Asia from a real expert.

Paul Taylor
Vice President and General Counsel
Ajinomoto North America

Successful business experiences take on a differing dimension around the globe. Learning the rules of the game is far more complex in another culture where words and conduct may have opposite meaning than expected. Managing in Asia identifies those historical and cultural factors crucial to success from concept to negotiation to management.

Elaine Marshall
North Carolina Secretary of State, 1997–present

Managing in Asia

Mastering Asia's Divergent Management Practices

Robert Charles Azar

Books may be purchased in quantity by contacting the publisher at info@writewaypublishing.com.

Printed in the United States of America
ISBN 978-1-946425-71-3

Cover Design by CSinclaire Write-Design
Book Design by CSinclaire Write-Design

WRITEWAY
PUBLISHING

Other Books by the Author

Negotiating in Asia

A Practical Guide to Succeeding in International Negotiation

An analysis of how and why negotiating is conducted differently between the West and Asia and among the major economies of Asia

Navigating Japan's Business Culture

A Practical Guide to Succeeding in the Japanese Market

An in-depth case study analysis of the challenges that international executives confront in managing business with the primary economic and geopolitical partner for the U.S. in Asia

Insightful Thoughts for the Journey Through Life

Original and uplifting life affirmations that combine Eastern wisdom and Western philosophy

CONTENTS

INTRODUCTION

Today Asia accounts for approximately half of total global GDP. The World Economic Forum estimates the region's share will increase to sixty percent by 2030, with three of the world's four largest economies being in Asia by 2040—China, Japan, and India. While Asia's economies and companies command such a dominating role and importance in international business to an ever-greater degree, the West's understanding of the region's divergent business practices and how to effectively manage within them has not increased in a commensurate manner.

Specifically, the approach, logic, goals, priorities, and methods of business utilized in that region differ significantly from those in the West. The result is an uneven playing field in which American and European companies—and governments—are at a distinct disadvantage both strategically and tactically when dealing with their Asian counterparts. Two recent and representative examples are the U.S. government's inability to successfully negotiate a meaningful solution to its trade dispute with China and the West being caught off guard by China's initial handling of the COVID-19 pandemic, as we shall discuss.

Just how different are Asia's management practices from those of the West? Honda Soichiro, the founder and CEO of the Honda Motor Corporation, unequivocally described the differences when he stated that they differ in all their important aspects:

> *Japanese and American management styles are 95 percent the same—and different in all important aspects.* —**Honda Soichiro, Founder and CEO, Honda Motor Co., Ltd.** (accessed April 28, 2021). ***http://www.quoteswise.com/soichiro-honda-quotes-3.html.***

Applying far beyond the U.S. and Japan, Mr. Honda's comparison is true for markets and regions across the entire globe. This should not be surprising. According to Peter Drucker, the founder of modern Western principles of management, it is a requirement that any country combines capitalism with its own indigenous cultural values and social norms in order for a modern economy to succeed in that nation. Those indigenous cultural values and social norms are the very building blocks of each nation's management practices. Noted Dr. Drucker:

> *Management . . . is deeply imbedded in culture. What managers do in West Germany, in the United Kingdom, in the United States, in Japan, or in Brazil is exactly the same. How they do it may be quite different. Thus one of the basic challenges managers in a developing country face is to find and identify those parts of their own tradition, history, and culture that can be used as management building blocks. The difference between Japan's economic success and India's relative backwardness is largely explained by the fact*

the Japanese managers were able to plant imported management concepts in their own cultural soil and make them grow. —**Peter F. Drucker, *The Essential Drucker* (New York: Harper Collins, 2001), page 11.**

Why are cultural and social factors the building blocks of the management practices and modern economic system in any country? Because they inform the outlook, approach, logic, priorities, goals, methods, and the bottom-line results of every company and economy. A market's culture-based business practices govern how companies operate internally and interact externally with their numerous stakeholders—including potential Western partners. They are, in effect, the unique rules of the road in each international market. As Warren Buffet observed: "*Culture, more than rule books, determines how an organization behaves.*"[1] Consequently, each nation has its own distinct variety of capitalism and management practices that govern its economy and businesses that are based on its social norms, cultural values, and historical experience.[2]

Given that differing management practices, cultural roots and drivers, and conflicting management priorities and dynamics regularly act as obstacles for companies engaging in business internationally, is it possible for companies to proactively and strategically leverage those differences to maximize their success around the globe? The answer is definitely yes for the informed international executive. By taking the time to understand and adequately take the differences into account, the properly prepared

1 Accessed April 28, 2021. https://www.suredividend.com/warren-buffett-quotes/#management.

2 Robert Charles Azar. *Navigating Japan's Business Culture.* Chapter five offers an in-depth analysis of how Japan's social norms, cultural values, and historical experience were combined with Western capitalism, resulting in that nation's unique brand of capitalism and management practices.

multinational business can turn the difficulties those differences ordinarily present into a tactical advantage to maximize their bottom-line results and better secure their long-term interests. This book addresses these concerns with a three-pronged approach:

- Identifying comparative differences in major management practices between Asia and the West
- Explaining the cultural and social underpinnings and contexts of those differences so that international executives can accurately understand the underlying building blocks of management practices in those markets
- Offering practical, proven strategies and tactics for constructively dealing with these divergent management practices gained by this author through four decades of firsthand experience setting up and managing businesses in Asian markets for American and European clients

In the early 1980s, I began my career in international business, working for Asian companies in management positions. Right away I was captivated by how the logic, priorities, goals, approach, and the very methods of management differ from Western practices. These divergent facets of management are numerous, diverse, and far-reaching. Following is a list of thirty fundamental aspects of management that differ between these two regions:

1. Purpose of a corporation
2. Management priorities

3. Goals of management
4. Company's role in and relationship to society
5. Stakeholder obligation
6. Time frame governing management
7. Notions of time in management
8. Manner of decision-making
9. Style of management
10. Management tactics
11. Change management
12. Attitude toward risk
13. Rationale and logic used in management
14. Criteria for hiring
15. Employee management
16. Promotion practices
17. Management's responsibilities to employees
18. Business leadership
19. Significance and role of relationship
20. Relationship dynamics between companies
21. Relationship dynamics between departments or affiliates within a corporation
22. Business partnership management
23. Customer service standards and expectations
24. Product quality standards
25. View and role of business contracts
26. Meaning and function of "agreement"
27. Communication dynamics and their implications
28. Company-Government relationship and interaction
29. Nation's economic system demands on corporate management
30. Preference for raising capital through debt rather than equities

As a consequence of the need to understand and navigate the diverse management practices and requirements of global markets, managing internationally is significantly more complex than managing in one's domestic market. If managing domestically is equivalent to playing traditional two-dimensional chess, then managing internationally is akin to playing multi-dimensional chess with its greater number of layers, degrees of insight and strategic calculation, and number of items that need to be factored in to succeed.

The generic challenges that companies face when managing business in any foreign market—such as differences in levels of economic development, regulatory requirements, exchange rate fluctuations—are universal and not covered in this book. Those items are already well known and for the most part understood by international executives. Instead, this book gives special attention to the difficulties of managing business internationally that arise from culture-based differences in business practices—those building blocks of management referred to by Dr. Drucker. In my experience, culture-based differences in management are one of the primary causes for companies not achieving their full potential as they internationalize their business, often because executives generally are unaware of them, let alone know what to do to ameliorate them. This book aims to resolve much of this handicap by raising awareness and providing actionable solutions.

As noted from Dr. Drucker's quote above, markets throughout the world by necessity have management practice differences that arise from what he further refers to as their unique and diverse traditional "cultural soil." What, then, is that indigenous "cultural soil" in the case of Asian economies? What comprises it? How does it impact the way business is managed in that region? What challenges do these differing components present to foreign executives managing in Asian markets? How can non-native companies effectively deal with these differences to minimize negative consequences? Even more important is how can international executives proactively leverage these differences to maximize their success in markets around the globe?

This third book in my series on succeeding in international business in Asia identifies and explains many of the culture-based business practices that inform Asia's divergent management practices and answers each of the questions posed above.[3] This is a hands-on manual for executives wishing to succeed in managing their business in Asia-Pacific markets. It is designed to serve as a practical guide for understanding and successfully navigating the numerous obstacles that management practice differences present on the executive and operational levels on both a day-to-day and long-term basis.

By way of clarification, when I refer to culture, I do not mean aspects of the humanities. Rather for the purposes of my work, culture is defined as the sensibilities of the people; the preferences of the society; and the customary norms by which the people live, view the world, prioritize, make decisions, interact with each other within a group, and engage with other groups. These encompass the outlooks and values that people in any society are subconsciously socialized with and live by. In the area of international business, they inform the fundamental building blocks of management and how businesses are run in each country around the world.

3 For the purposes of this book, Asia is defined as the Asia-Pacific region, incorporating northeast and southeast Asia and excluding India, the rest of southwest Asia, Australia, and New Zealand.

These sensibilities, preferences, and norms bring with them their own complex web of cultural nuances, subconscious outlooks, unspoken expectations, differing logic, and built-in requirements that are unique to each market. This is especially true in the distinct cultural context of Asian business. This book identifies those fundamentals in that region, explaining their cultural roots, how they inform the way Asian executives manage and engage in business, the resulting challenges they present to foreign companies, and how Western executives can most effectively navigate them.

Ten years of formal academic training and field research in Asian political, economic, and cultural affairs at New York University and Columbia University; post-graduate studies in international management, global marketing, and business law at Harvard University; forty years of hands-on, executive-level experience in managing business operations between Asia and the West; seven years of full-time living and working in the Far East; an additional fifteen years of accumulated time residing and working in the region; over one million flight miles flown to, from, and within Asia in service of clients; fluency in reading, writing, and speaking the Japanese language; familiarity with the Chinese and Korean languages; and a lifetime of study have made it abundantly clear to me that there is one overwhelming reason why Western companies either do not achieve their full potential or outright fail in Asian markets. That reason is ultimately the inability to recognize, understand, and effectively deal with culture-based differences in management building blocks and practices. It is essential that effectively navigating these differences needs to be a priority task within every firm's international management as the case studies and numerous client experiences throughout this book demonstrate.

The influence of cultural factors on management must not be underestimated. This book contains dozens of examples of how divergent management practices and their underlying social dynamics directly impede the bottom-line performance and long-term interests of companies in international business. This is not simply an Asia-West issue. Robert Lutz, former Vice Chairman of the Chrysler Corporation, noted the prominent role culture-based differences played in the failure of the DaimlerChrysler merger. He stated that it was the cultural difference that made it hard to achieve the synergies that had been the great attraction of the deal.[4] Differences in business culture and their accompanying management practices prevented these two major, well-experienced international corporations from succeeding in their merger and cost them billions of dollars.

Generic challenges in international business that are readily understood by international business professionals are akin to the proverbial tip of the iceberg that is seen and recognized while the culture-based obstacles are the part of the iceberg below the surface. International executives often operate only seeing the tip of the iceberg and miss the dangers of the stealth presence of the culture-based factors below. These behind-the-scene business dynamics are ever-present, but not seen, not known, and therefore not understood. As a consequence, international managers often operate in the dark and unknowingly shortchange their results in international business.

While most books available in America on the subject of doing business in Asia deal with the etiquette of Asian societies,

4 *Automotive News*. "The DaimlerChrysler Merger: The culture clash heard 'round the world." May 6, 2018. accessed June 4, 2020. http://www.autonews.com/article/20180507/FEATURE/180509923/the-culture-clash-heard-round-the-world.

these rules of social etiquette are not core aspects of management or business. Likewise, books on cultural intelligence (CQ) tend to focus on cultural competence theory—namely, paradigms regarding how to describe the cultural traits of a foreign market. For example, is communication high or low context? Or is decision-making top down or bottom up? While theories and paradigms of cultural intelligence are helpful by providing *descriptions*, this book provides real, *actionable insights, strategies, and tactics*.

I refer to this as *intercultural management* as it identifies differences in culture, how those differences impact business, and what management can do to operate their business most effectively in light of them. The goal of this book is for culture-based differences in management practices to no longer to be obstacles to companies working to achieve their business objectives abroad—in short, to prevent cultural borders from acting as business barriers. Furthermore, once aware of these cultural dynamics informing management practices, international executives can for the first time leverage them strategically to enhance their success.

The information contained in this book is factual and was learned through personal experience engaging in business between Asia and the West over the course of my career. The names of companies, employees, and products of Western and Asian firms that I worked with have been changed out of respect for their privacy; however, the names of historical companies and individuals have not.

The aim of this book is to illuminate and explain the mainstream business practices of Asia's indigenous management culture. The nations of Asia are at different levels of internationalizing and incorporating Western management outlooks and practices. As American and European executives are obviously already accustomed to Western management, this book focuses on Asia's indigenous management practices–that part of the equation of conducting business in Asia that is not well-understood outside the region.

While indigenous Asian management practices are the focus of this book, they are obviously not the only type of management practices in the region. Individual nations in Asia also operate with differing degrees of international management practices; Singapore is characterized more by international business practices than Vietnam, for example. In the same manner, differences in the degree of indigenous management practices versus international practices that Western firms experience will vary within each Asian market from industry to industry, company to company, and individual to individual, depending on the degree of internationalization. Chapter five discusses the six major factors that determine whether the management practices Western companies will experience in each unique Asian market are informed more by indigenous or international norms.

This book will be of interest to and benefit three groups of readers: individuals with professional interests in international management, those with an academic interest in Asia, and the culturally curious and globally minded who are interested in the many diverse cultures that enrich our world. It is my hope that this book will help improve international business and understanding of the management fundamentals that underpin it, thereby promoting greater stability, cooperation, and prosperity in the twenty-first century.

Robert Charles Azar
December 2021

PART 1

FUNDAMENTALS OF ASIAN MANAGEMENT

Managing Companies, Partners, Customers

Chapter 1

MANAGING COMPANIES: *Social Foundations*

Business partners are those who are often sleeping in the same bed but having different dreams.—**Chinese anonymous**

While this traditional Chinese proverb is true between domestic companies in that market, it is exponentially more apropos for Western firms conducting business with local companies throughout the Asian region. Companies engaged in international business together may be committed to the same shared business goals and yet at the same time have views, strategies, expectations, and practices regarding that same business that are quite different from each other.

Western and Asian business partners commonly have divergent priorities, goals, approaches, rationales, logic, and practices that they utilize in pursing shared business objectives. How, specifically, do these fundamentals that govern management differ? What is their impact on day-to-day management methods and bottom-line results? What obstacles inherent in them challenge American and European firms? Most importantly, how can international executives successfully navigate and leverage these divergencies to conduct business in Asia more adeptly?

Part one of this book addresses these topics as they relate to managing one's company, business partners, customers, and employees in Asian markets. Chapter one begins this discussion by analyzing Asia's indigenous management practices for running companies.

I. DIVERGENT APPROACHES, RATIONALES, AND LOGIC IN MANAGEMENT

My client and I had just finished five-and-a-half hours of meetings with a Shanghai-based prospective partner. In the taxi ride back to our hotel, Victoria Olbrich, Vice President of Alamance Corporation, was perplexed as she remarked, "We just spent almost the entire day having in-depth discussion with the executives of this Chinese firm we are interested in working with and didn't reach agreement on many major points. It seems as though we went around and around and spoke about so many topics that were unrelated. I'm now wondering what it was all for." Jonathan Thompson, Alamance's President and CEO, nodded in agreement and asked, "What just happened in there, Robert? I feel we achieved very little today."

This reaction is quite understandable among international executives engaging in business in Asia. While it is certainly a fair observation from a Western perspective, from an Asian vantage point nothing could be further from what actually transpired. The Alamance executives experienced a different perspective on expectations for their meeting. This differing perspective will become clearer as we continue.

This experience highlights a profound difference in the conduct of business in the world's two major economic regions. It points out the fact that the two areas utilize fundamentally different approaches, rationales, and types of logic in the conduct of management and business in general. These divergent fundamentals present major challenges to firms as they operate their business in Asian markets.

Most major regions and cultures of the world have their own indigenous way of looking at things and underlying logic, one that is grounded in their unique culture and that reflects the outlook, sensibilities, values, priorities, and expectations of its people, societies, companies, and governments. The challenge for executives managing in international business is that these different approaches, rationales, and logic are usually incongruous with those they are accustomed to in their home markets.

This clash is ever present in international management. Sometimes it operates as the submerged part of the proverbial iceberg, impeding both the speed and scope of a company's progress. At other times it is impacts business quite visibly above the surface, playing out right out in the open, causing an erosion of trust and confidence in one's Asian partner, limiting a firm's business performance, or causing it to outright fail. In either case, the clash of differing fundamentals in international management is profound and perpetual. It affects management practices that govern most facets of business—including goal setting, time horizons, strategy formulation, levels of financial investment, execution tactics, negotiation, decision-making, relationship dynamics, human resource development, leadership, sales and marketing, customer service, and bottom-line management.

Let's take a closer look at these differing types of logic in Western and Asian management and the resulting dissimilar approaches, priorities, and practices in management in both regions. This information applies to both the internal and external practices of a business.

While Western civilization focuses on the primacy and importance of the individual, Asian culture has traditionally been collectivistic with the group being the center of one's orientation. That applies whether the group is one's family, community, company, or nation. While the individual is seen as being autonomous and self-reliant in America and Europe, in Asia members of the group are viewed as being interconnected and mutually dependent. While Western logic, cultural values, and social expectations emphasize what is best for individual interest, Asia's rationale prioritizes what is in the interest of the group or collectivist whole. While Western companies drill down on specific *individual* parts or specific items of a situation in a linear fashion, Asian firms focus on the *entirety* of the situation and take an integrated or holistic approach—often misperceived as going around and around discussing seemingly unrelated topics, as noted by the Alamance Corporation executives.

Morita Akio, the Sony Corporation's co-founder and President, summarized this difference in holistic management logic between Asia and the West this way:

> *Instead of juxtaposing facts, they [Asian management] look at an idea from a holistic point of view. . . . So they have a better grasp of the [whole integrated] situation than someone who sees it only in parts.*— **(accessed April 19, 2021)** ***www.quoteswise.com/akio-morita-quotes-2.html***

The contrast between Asia's holistic and the West's individual part approach is clearly seen in the divergent business models that IT companies have used in developing their business in those regions. See Appendix 4 for details of the fundamental difference in this management building block.

When approaching matters in the West, we do so in what we deem to be a logical manner with a rational order and linear logic. In Asia, matters are approached with a more holistic manner that often seems incongruous to what is considered to be logical in the West. Corporate decisions are not always based on the same hard and fast, by the numbers, bottom line calculation of profit. Other goals and priorities inform the logic and decisions of Asian management as discussed throughout this book.

To offer a quick example, I have witnessed countless times throughout the region business decisions being made not based on what is best for the company's bottom line as is typically the definitive standard in the West, but rather what is best for the relationship of the companies involved in the business and the overall situation. Management would select an option that was clearly understood to provide a lower return on investment but regardless of that, it was in the better interest of the mutual relationship and business. This dynamic illustrates the priority given the interests of the integrated whole over those of the individual parties.

Often decisions by managers in the West are made by one department that may not be favorable to other parts of the company. It is not unusual for decisions made by one department not even to be discussed with other departments that will be affected by them. In the holistic logic of management in Asia, all impacted departments within the company are involved in the decision-making process. Within this holistic logic, Asian executives weigh the following seven parameters in discussions, decision-making, strategy formulation, and implementation of management policies:

- The immediate item under discussion
- The risks and rewards of the specific project or business situation at hand
- The short-term impact on the entire company
- The long-term consequences for the firm, including all its departments and stakeholders
- The impact on the business relationships between the companies involved
- The greater interests of the company beyond the specific business matter under discussion and how those interests will be impacted by the matter
- The company's societal obligation and standing

While the first three of these factors are likewise taken into consideration by Western management, the remaining four are typically not given the same weight as in Asia. The last one, a company's societal obligation, has only recently started to become an important consideration in Western management practices. Likewise, while government required goals and management practices placed on companies are a feature of the state-controlled economies of China and Vietnam as well as of the society-oriented economies of most other Asian nations, they typically are not present in the non-collectivist management of most Western nations.

Asia's holistic outlook is the result of the world view of two major forces that have shaped the cultures, value systems, social organization, educational systems, government, and economic structures of societies in the region for centuries: Confucianism and Taoism. Both of these social philosophies stress the following points:

- Each individual is but one small part of the greater whole.

- All entities are mutually connected and interdependent. Actions taken by one party affect the others one is connected with. Since all parties are dependent on their mutual relationships, taking a comprehensive approach rather than focusing on individual aspects is natural.

- The relationships connecting all things are of utmost importance and priority. Proper balance and collaborative relationships (harmony) between all entities are of greatest significance and are to be maintained at all times. Consequently, all decisions must be mutually beneficial, not favoring just one party.

This outlook of mutual connection and interdependence has the greatest importance in the region in Japan due to the additional and reinforcing influence of that nation's native Shinto religion. The importance of mutual connection, interdependence, and the relationships that sustain them are so important that Shinto teaches that salvation is attained not in the afterlife as in Western religions but in this life by maintaining harmonious relationships and fulfilling one's duties to others regarding them.[5]

The notion of mutual connection and primacy of relationship is one of the main pillars of Asia's collectivist societies and is fundamental to the approach, rationale, and logic of management practices in the region.

The COVID-19 pandemic provides an excellent example of this different approach, rationale, and logic between the West and Asia, especially regarding sheltering at home and wearing face masks.

Sheltering at home is universally disliked around the world, but the differing response to it illustrates the fundamental difference in individual versus collectivist outlook and practices of the two regions. Understanding that it is in the *better interests of society at large*, it was accepted and complied with in Asia. In the U.S., in contrast, there was push back against it from many who claim that it violated their *individual rights*.

We see the same regarding the wearing of face masks. Their use in Asia has been common practice for over a century,

5 For an in-depth case study analysis of mutual connection, interdependence, primacy of relationship, and holistic logic and their influence on modern business practices in the world's third largest economy, see Robert Charles Azar, *Navigating Japan's Business Culture: A Practical Guide to Succeeding in the Japanese Market.*

a permanent lesson adopted from the Spanish flu pandemic of 1918. It has become common practice for individuals to automatically wear a mask as soon as they start to catch a cold or the flu. They do so not to protect themselves—they have already become sick. They do so to protect those around them, an example of the collectivist values and society-oriented outlook of the region.

In the West, such a society-oriented practice does not exist, and individuals who believe they are not at risk to contract COVID-19 simply refuse to wear any face coverings or to socially distance. Their thinking is clearly individual-oriented and lacks consideration for those around them or society at large. In the U.S., some citizens protesting mask wearing have gone so far as to cite one of the battle cries of America's War of Independence from Britain: "Give me liberty or give me death." Responses to the pandemic illustrate how fundamentally different values, priorities, and practices are in the two regions.

It is through the collectivist lens of this macro level outlook that Asian executives view and manage business. How fundamental and far-reaching are the divergent approaches, rationales, and logic? Also noted in the Introduction, the following is a representative list of thirty facets of management that differ between the West and Asia as a result of them:

1. Purpose of a corporation
2. Management priorities
3. Goals of management
4. Company's role in and relationship to society
5. Stakeholder obligation
6. Time frame governing management
7. Notions of time in management

8. Manner of decision-making
9. Style of management
10. Management tactics
11. Change management
12. Attitude toward risk
13. Rationale and logic used in management
14. Criteria for hiring
15. Employee management
16. Promotion practices
17. Management's responsibilities to employees
18. Business leadership
19. Significance and role of relationship
20. Relationship dynamics between companies
21. Relationship dynamics between departments or affiliates within a corporation
22. Business partnership management
23. Customer service standards and expectations
24. Product quality standards
25. View and role of business contracts
26. Meaning and function of "agreement"
27. Communication dynamics and their implications
28. Company-government relationship and interaction
29. Nation's economic system demands on corporate management
30. Preference for raising capital through debt rather than equities

For a more detailed analysis of Asia's holistic logic and management, refer to Appendix Three.

II. CONTRASTING PRIORITIES AND GOALS IN MANAGEMENT

Based on the differing approaches, rationales, and logic used in management, Asian firms operate with priorities, goals, and purpose of management that are often dissimilar from those in the West. They represent an ever-present and far-reaching challenge for non-native companies. Let's start with the example of different time horizons that govern management. These apply to both executive and day-to-day management practices.

A. VARYING TIME PERSPECTIVES

Comparatively speaking, Western executives view, approach, plan, execute, and review business on a shorter-term basis. The performances of individual employees, company departments, and the corporation itself are evaluated and, when warranted, rewarded based on shorter term results. This is best epitomized by Wall Street where corporations and their management in all industries are evaluated based on quarterly profit performance.

In contrast, Asian executives generally employ a longer-term perspective in operating their businesses. Rather than managing focused on results on a quarterly or yearly basis, Asian firms give greater weight to achieving positive returns over the long term, with long term being measured in multiple years.

I first experienced this in the 1980s when I was working as a financial analyst and political economist on Wall Street with Daiwa Securities, Inc. in their North American headquarters located in the World Financial Center in New York City. At the time, Daiwa was Japan's—and the world's—second largest investment firm. It was fascinating to observe how financial reports on companies and industries written by my Japanese coworkers at Daiwa consistently covered a significantly longer time horizon than reports on the same topics written by American colleagues working in Goldman Sachs, Merrill Lynch, and other prominent U.S. investment firms. While evaluating quarterly and one-to-three-year performance results, my coworkers also analyzed and gave greater weight to each company's or industry's long-term performance, typically five- and ten-year results.

Later in my career, when I set up and managed the businesses of American and European clients in Asia through my management consulting practice, I experienced firsthand just how different these time horizons guiding the practice of management are in Asia and the West.

A common area of this difference in management's time horizon is how investment and profit are prioritized. Compared to American and European businesses, it is common for Asian firms to invest more upfront to maximize the project's launch and lay the foundation to gain long-term value creation and market share sustainability, even though that usually means less profit in the short term. The Toyota Motor Corporation, one of Asia's first corporations to become a global powerhouse, for example, consistently operates with this approach. As Kamiya Shotaro, a native Japanese and former assistant manager of General Motors Japan who moved to Toyota where his approach to management was compatible with the firm's, stated:

> *The company's business would come to a halt if we concentrated exclusively on latent [customer] demand for today and tomorrow. We have to think five and ten years out and work to expand latent demand*

on that scale. We must do it, even at the expense of immediate profit. —**Hino, Satoshi. *Inside The Mind of Toyota: Management Principles for Enduring Growth.* New York: Productivity Press, 2006, page 12.**

Why is it that management practices in Asia give such importance and priority to the long term? The reason stems from the divergent goals of management in the two regions. The goal of management is not primarily profit as in the West; instead, greater priority for sustainable long-term value creation and market share has traditionally been the norm.

The rationale for this management practice is that long-term market share is viewed as providing long-term stability of revenues and profits for the company's bottom line and for advancing its overall business interests. This stability enables management to plan, invest, and execute such items as product development, R&D, employee training, finances, quality assurance, and customer relationship management at a greater level over the long term. Long-term, stable revenues and profit allow for long-term, stable value creation and success.

Not only does management in Asia and the West operate based on different time horizons, but the very meaning of time periods used in managing varies between the regions.

Not only does management in Asia and the West operate based on different time horizons, but the very meaning of time periods used in managing varies between the regions.

A client example from the early years of my management

consulting practice illustrates this intriguing difference.

I received a phone call in my New York office from Mr. Alexander, the president of a Beverly Hills-based client, on a Friday evening. He reported to me that nearly two months had already passed since starting the trial period of the sales project with our partner company in Asia, yet they were nowhere near the project's mutually agreed upon short-term sales levels. He added that if they didn't meet the goals soon, we would have to find a different partner in that market, and he requested that I go meet with the company and find out what the problem was.

At the meeting with our Asian partner, I discussed Mr. Alexander's concern. Their response was quite revealing. They questioned why Mr. Alexander was worried and why he was comparing the results after two months with our mutually agreed upon short-term goals. They added that their company was confident it was well on the way to achieving those goals.

When I replied that it had *already* been two months since starting, they responded, "Exactly, it has *only* been two months since starting." Through further discussion, it became clear that their meaning of "short term" was markedly different from that of my U.S. client and me.

As is common in the West, for Mr. Alexander short term was measured in months or quarters. Generally, in the West, short term is three to six or nine months. Mid-term often ranges anywhere from nine to eighteen months, while long term is anything beyond that. In contrast, short term for our Asian partner was one to two years, mid-term three to four years, and long term five or ten years. This time frame is typical in that region. Over the course of my career, it became clear that not only is Asian management based on a longer-term perspective but also the very definitions of short term, mid-term, and long term are significantly longer periods than in the West.

While management time horizons are longer in Asia than the West, generally speaking, they vary within the region. China, for example, employs the longest time horizons among Asian markets. It is common for executives there to work with business plans that go out ten years. One contributing reason for this is that since it embarked on its drive to industrialize in 1978 at the end of its Maoist period, China's central government follows medium range five-year plans for developing and managing the nation's industry and economy and ten-year plans that establish the country's long-term direction and strategic objectives. Consequently, the management practices of the country's largest corporations, the majority of which are now or started out as state-owned enterprises, likewise cover similarly long periods.

This same long-term time horizon has been utilized in Vietnam since it began its industrialization drive. The nation's economy was a state run, centrally planned socialist economy from 1976 to 1986 when the country began to shift to a mixed economy—or a "socialist-oriented market economy" (*doi moi*), as it is referred to locally.

In contrast, however, it is noteworthy that while this long-time horizon applies to large corporations in Korea, it is quite a different story when it comes to small and middle-sized companies. They are at the other end of the time horizon spectrum. They constantly seek to accelerate the pace of business and want everything to move as quickly as possible—whether it is negotiating, planning, launching the business, turning a profit, or other facets of management.

The Korean phrase commonly used for accelerating the pace is *ppalli ppalli* (빨리빨리), literally meaning "quickly, quickly." *Ppalli ppalli* is comparable in nuance to the American phrase "get it done yesterday." Numerous times I experienced firsthand this *ppalli ppalli* dynamic in the Korean market.

Often my initial meeting on behalf of clients with potential business partners there would include a presentation on the background of my American or European client company, the products they wanted to sell in Korea, the strategy behind the marketing plan for the Korean market, and how Korea fit into the client's global business strategy. When I would be only forty or fifty percent of the way through the initial presentation, it was common for a senior Korean executive to interrupt me and say, "Thank you for the presentation. We definitely want to sell those products in Korea. Let's sign your sales agreement now." I would invariably reply that I hadn't finished the presentation yet. Their response generally went along the lines of "That's okay. We can see this is a big opportunity, and we want it. Let's get started *very quickly (ppalli ppalli)*!"

While fast-paced discussions, decision-making, and strategy execution among small and medium-sized Korean businesses are quite refreshing to Western companies after the often painfully slow pace of discussions and negotiations in other Asian markets, this dynamic nonetheless contains huge risks. International executives need to be aware of this problematic practice and its negative consequences:

- Incomplete preparation work for new business operations
- Salient facets of your business overlooked or otherwise falling through the cracks
- Projects executed without sufficient management oversight, corporate investment, employee understanding, or effectiveness

Another risk is that your business partner in the Korean market will walk away from your business just as quickly as they got on board, leaving you to salvage your Korean operations either by starting all over again to find a local partner or cutting your losses and leaving one of the region's most lucrative markets. Given this management dynamic, international executives should not be surprised when commitments and plans end up being half-baked or short-lived.

Japan, Indonesia, Malaysia, Singapore, Taiwan, Thailand, and Vietnam lie in between China and Korea in terms of time horizons. Excluding Korea, in Asian markets negotiations are longer and business proceeds more slowly comparatively speaking than in the West, but the advantage is the resulting collaboration is typically stronger and longer term. This is most pronounced in Japan given the different meaning and level of importance of relationship in business.

The difference between management based on a short-term profit focus in the West versus a long-term growth and stability orientation in Asia is rooted in the *divergent collectivist values* that serve as management building blocks in the latter region. As Dr. Drucker observed:

In any conflict between short-term results and long-term growth, one company decides in favor of long-term growth, another company decides such a conflict in favor of short-term results. Again this is not primarily a disagreement on economics. It is fundamentally a **value conflict** *regarding the function of a business and the responsibilities of management.* [bold in original text] —**Peter F. Drucker, "Managing Oneself" in *Management.*** (accessed April 28, 2021) ***https://www.mbiconcepts.com/ibm-and-peter-f-drucker-first-article.html***

The significantly different time perspectives governing management in Asia and the West are illustrated in the following figure.

Figure 1: Short-Term vs. Long-Term Perspective in Management

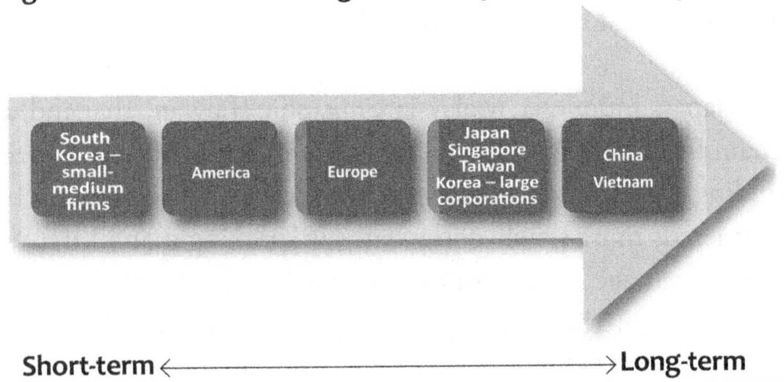

Source: Robert Charles Azar, 2021

Another cultural factor underpinning the region's long-term vantage is the significantly longer histories that Asian nations enjoy compared to the U.S. While America is approaching its two-hundred-and-fiftieth birthday, China's time line is

6,000 years long; Korea's is 4,000 years; and Japan's is 2,000 years. Executives throughout Asia have never hesitated to point out this fact to me. With this historical context in mind, I appreciated how, when discussing management time perspectives in China, I have often been told by executives that "for Chinese, long term is measured in generations—not in years."

It is critically important that Western executives keep this difference in management time perspectives in mind when operating their firms as well as managing their business relationships with partners in Asia. For their part, Asian executives need to see that a Western company is likewise committed to working together for the long term and is willing to make decisions based on what is in the long-term—not just short-term—interests of the project. This can entail foregoing greater profits in the short term for the sake of the long-term benefits of the joint business.

In light of this, it is strongly recommended that international executives early on discuss and come to agreement with their Asian partners what balance between these two management time horizons will govern their mutual business project. It is critically important that you confirm this agreement not just for the short term but for all stages of your business.

B. CONTRASTING MANAGEMENT PRIORITIES AND GOALS

Inherent in these different time perspectives are divergent management priorities and goals. In order to meet short-term profit and stock price targets, Western—especially American—management frequently and matter-of-factly engages in numerous corporate actions such as:

- Employee layoffs.
- Price reductions.
- Aggressive promotional programs.
- Reduction or cancellation of investment in plant, equipment, research and development, new product launches, and business expansion.
- Company divisions, subsidiaries, or other affiliates being sold off.
- Physical and financial asset liquidation.

Divergent management practices are characteristic within different time perspectives.

Asian executives are bewildered by these management practices, especially how in the U.S. employees are laid off not after a recession has actually begun but when it seems one may be looming. Laying off workers in preparation for an apparent recession is seen as actually hastening or even contributing to the start of one. These cost cutting measures to attain short-term profit goals are viewed in Asia as detrimental to the firm's long-term well-being, stability, performance, and profits.

Furthermore, this short-term perspective is viewed negatively because it does not recognize and factor in the long-term value of the company's assets—especially employees who accumulate decades of experience, insights, and relationships in their industry that cannot be easily replaced.

One advantage of the West's short-term approach is that companies are able to reduce expenses quickly when confronting a recession or a major decline in corporate revenues. This enables management to be nimbler and more responsive to downturns in business. The fact that American companies were able to return to profitability after the Great Recession of 2008—and almost all other economic downturns in recent history—more quickly than companies around the world is evidence that this approach has its merits.

The advantage of Asia's approach is that management is less beholden to short-term returns or the interests of shareholders and is able to focus on the long-term well-being and performance of the company. This also underlies the preference of management to raise capital through corporate debt rather than equities; they are more able to focus on long-term interests even at the expense of short-term profitability. By way of example, this management approach is crystallized—and prioritized—in the very first section of the Toyota Motor Corporation's business principles entitled "*Executive Summary of the 14 Toyota Way Principles*":

Section 1: Long-Term Philosophy.

Principle 1. Base your management decisions on a long-term philosophy, even at the expense of short-term financial goals. —**Liker, Jeffrey K. *The Toyota Way: 14 Management Principles from the World's Greatest Manufacturer*. New York: McGraw-Hill, 2004. Page 37.**

Western, especially American, companies are known for not hesitating to discontinue a business venture if it does not meet short term targets. Asian firms are generally more willing to let a venture with weaker than expected initial performance continue longer before making any terminating decisions.

While the "cut your losses" approach to management commonplace in America and Europe makes sense from the perspective of Western logic and other management fundamentals, it runs contrary to the way business is traditionally conducted in Asian markets. It bewilders employees, weakening their confidence in and commitment to management and the company. The result is a less motivated and productive work force as well as lower financial performance for the corporation.

> The "cut your losses" approach to management commonplace in America and Europe runs contrary to the way business is traditionally conducted in Asian markets.

From the Asian perspective, the concern about differing priorities and goals is especially strong regarding small and medium-sized Western firms that Asian companies may work with as these firms typically do not have the same resources and staying power as large corporations to stick it out if sales turn out to be slower than initially expected. I have often heard Asian executives say that if a small or medium-sized company is going to be "here today, gone tomorrow" because sales are below expectations for a few quarters, why even bother to start the business. It turns out to be a waste of time, effort, and investment for both companies. This is further problematic in Asia as it often causes companies "to lose face" on two levels:

- **In their industry among their peer companies**

  Prestige and perceived standing among their competitors often suffer as a result of come and go associations.

- **With the public and society in general**

  The exit of foreign companies can leave the Asian company in a difficult situation. Officially they are no longer engaged in that business and have ceased those operations. However, the company can remain socially obligated to continue servicing customers who have purchased those products after the foreign company has left. It becomes highly problematic and costly to handle customer inquiries, complaints, maintenance, warranty issues, after-purchase product service needs, and repairs with no back up from the foreign manufacturer and no sales income from that project.

These concerns are another example of the greater societal orientation and obligations of business in the region and are among the reasons why Asian companies want to see that the management of an international partner company is committed to their market for the long term.

In citing a recent example from Singapore, in 2019 Mr. Loh Boon Chye, CEO of the Singapore Exchange (the nation's main stock exchange), described how management's responsibility is to manage and create value with a long-term perspective even if done at the expense of short-term benefit:

> *Boards need to think of growing company value and passing it to the next generation of shareholders. This also means making business decisions whose benefits may sometimes not be immediately apparent or are unpopular.*—**Loh Boon Chye. "Taking a long-term view." The Business Times. July 28, 2019.** (accessed April 29, 2021) ***https://www.businesstimes.com.sg/opinion/taking-a-long-term-view***

Notice that the CEO of the Singapore Exchange describes long term as generational, not as quarters or a few years.

A recent survey of major Chinese corporations conducted by the CPP Investment Board, a professional investment management organization, illustrates this preference in Asian management for a long-term orientation and creating stable, long-term corporate value. The study surveyed 180 major publicly listed Chinese companies that operate in 28 industries. They included both state-owned and non-state-owned firms and have a total market capitalization of $2.41 trillion—approximately one quarter of China's total stock market capitalization. As the survey results indicate, companies place heavy emphasis on long-term planning and value creation. Specific findings include:

- 89% of companies report valuing long-term, stable leadership for their businesses.

- 80% of surveyed companies state they take a long-term view and have strategic plans for long-term value creation.

- 70% of companies indicated their long-term strategic plans are either moderately or well defined.

- 70% of firms have medium- to long-term valuation metrics and road maps for achieving long-term plans established and in place.

- 70% of companies tie executive remuneration to long-term value creation.

When asked if they would delay a project that had long-term value for their company but could potentially also have a negative impact on reaching a short-term earnings target, only 18 percent of those companies said they would delay the project. In contrast, 50 percent of corporations in other global markets replied they would delay such a project that would negatively impact shot-term earnings goals.[6]

What consequence does this have for international firms

6 (Accessed April 29, 2021) https://www.cppib.com/en/public-media/headlines/2017/chinese-companies-longer-term-strategies/

managing their business operations in Asian markets? It is necessary for the firms to take into account the long-term perspective and the resulting divergent management priorities and goals of management in the region. This includes:

- Long-term planning, investing, and execution.
- Priority given to stable, long-term profit, value creation, and market share in addition to short-term performance and evaluation.
- A greater degree of patience regarding below-expectation performance.
- Stable corporate management, leadership, and intercompany relationships in pursuing the long-term, value creation, and market share goals of management.

Long-term return on investment in Asia requires Western executives to discuss and come to agreement with partners in the region on which of these divergent time horizons, goals, and priorities will govern their joint business. It is imperative to clarify which management fundamentals will be utilized in any collaboration at the outset of business discussions so the ground rules for the mutual business are clear and agreed upon.

These fundamental differences between the divergent priorities and goals of Western and Asian management are depicted in the following figure.

Figure 2: Divergent Priorities and Goals of Management

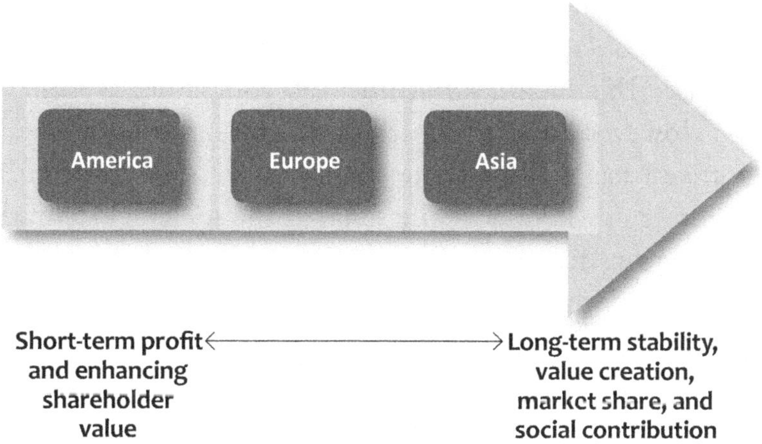

Source: Robert Charles Azar, 2021

Differences in management perspectives and goals impact far more than the time horizons and priorities discussed in this section. As we will see, they result in divergent practices in most areas of business in Asia.

III. SOCIETAL ORIENTATION AND MANAGEMENT PRACTICES

As the over-riding focus of management in Western firms is corporate profitability, companies pursue their bottom-line interests with high priority. Regarding contributing to society at large, they have traditionally been free to elect if, when, and to what degree they do so. When they do, it typically has taken the form of being a good corporate citizen and contributing to specific organizations or activities in society, such as supporting the arts, an education program, a sports team, or a sports arena.

In recent years, the number of Western companies electing to focus on the "triple bottom line"—that is, the company's stakeholders, society at large, and the environment—has begun to increase. This includes Fortune 500 companies as well as B Corps. However, making contributions to societal activities on an elective basis and even the self-declared triple bottom line aspiration is nowhere near the same as the societal orientation and obligation that Asian firms possess. Nor is their influence on management priorities and practices near the impact level in Asia.

In Asia, societal orientation has a significantly more prominent and long-standing role in management and is part of a company's *raison d' etre*, one that transcends the notions of good corporate citizenship in the West. Asian businesses generally view it as part of their role to be of benefit to society at large. They do so in numerous ways, including:

- Providing the product or service they offer. While providing its product or service for profit is certainly part of a company's motivation, providing their product or service is also seen as an act to benefit society at large. This is part of their holistic outlook that all actors in society are interconnected and mutually dependent.

- Contributing to society by maintaining stable employment.

- Advancing their country's over-all well-being through their activities.

- Contributing to building their nation and economy through their work.

Major Western companies have generally not incorporated societal considerations in management decisions to a similar degree. European firms are further ahead in doing so than U.S. companies which have only recently started to respond favorably to outside pressure put on them by stakeholders advocating for environmental, social, and governance (ESG) issues.[7]

For example, younger customers use ESG considerations in purchasing decisions and are willing to pay a premium price for those products. Meanwhile, investors have started to utilize ESG criteria to evaluate companies for investing. As a result, ESG considerations are being debated to a greater degree in the board rooms of Western companies. Despite that, however, they have not become mainstream to the degree they are in Asia.

It is noteworthy to point out two fundamental differences in societal considerations. In the West, ESG concerns have typically been raised outside of companies by stakeholders who then put pressure on company management to factor them into their decision-making. This contrasts with Asian management that has proactively incorporated ESG matters into corporate decision-making and activities and has traditionally viewed them as intrinsic to a business.

Another point of difference between societal considerations is that the type of social issues that management focuses on

7 Harvard Law School Forum on Corporate Governance. "ESG + Incentives 2020 Report." (accessed April 21, 2021) https://corpgov.law.harvard.edu/2020/08/29/esg-incentives-2020-report/; McKinsey & Company. "The ESG premium: New perspectives on value and performance." February 2020. (accessed April 20, 2021) https://www.mckinsey.com/business-functions/sustainability/our-insights/the-esg-premium-new-perspectives-on-value-and-performance.

also differs between the West and Asia. In the States, for example, corporate social issues often deal with inequalities in American society—the gap in gender salary and career opportunity, racial diversification, and income inequalities, for example. In contrast, in Asia business dealings with social issues have focused on contributing to society's general welfare at large through providing stable employment and various forms of social aid, avoiding layoffs, and contributing to the greater needs of nation building, as discussed in section four of this chapter.

The impetus for pursuing society-benefiting actions also varies between the West and Asia. In the States, corporate management is pressured more and more to take positive actions in this regard because the risk and price for not doing so is rising; it could hurt the company's reputation, alienate customers and investors, hurt revenues, and negatively impact stock prices. Climate change, for instance, is being more broadly accepted by corporate management recently as a result of greater public pressure and management's awareness of the rising financial costs of its effects on business and the economy.

In short, Western management's interest in and actions regarding social issues have become a recent addition to corporate management as a means to protect their business, profit, and reputation. Management giving consideration to including ESG concerns in decisions is also in response to external pressure from various stakeholders. By way of contrast, management's societal orientation and nation building obligations in Asia have had social well-being as a fundamental purpose and motivation of management throughout each nation's process of industrialization. The following is a chronological list of six Asian countries and when they started their drive to industrialize and build a modern economy:

- Japan 1868
- Taiwan 1960s
- Singapore 1960s
- Korea 1960s
- China 1978
- Vietnam 1986

These differing notions of a company's relationship, role, and obligation to society are rooted in the historical experience of industrialization in the two regions. In the West, industrialization was spearheaded by the *private sector*—that is, individual industrialists and their companies (such as J.P. Morgan, John Rockefeller, and Andrew Carnegie in the U.S.). In contrast, in Asia the *public sector*—that is, government—led industrialization as part of their nation building process. This is the cause of the difference between the West's individual-focused, laissez-faire view of the relationship between government and business and Asia's holistic view that it is only natural that government, business, and academia cooperate together for the benefit of the entire nation and all its citizens. These two divergent perspectives are consistent with the origins of modern business in both regions.

Notions of a company's relationship, role, and obligation to society are rooted in the historical experience of industrialization in the two regions.

In the past, the U.S. and Europe have often criticized Asia's cooperation between government, business, and academia as being collusion, giving companies in that region an unfair advantage vis-à-vis Western firms. This was first directed at Japan in the 1980s with the term "Japan Inc."

China received the same criticism after it surpassed Japan to become the world's second largest economy in 2011 and began to economically challenge the West; it has been labeled "China Inc." From the perspective of Asian nations, however, it is completely natural for all three major sectors of society—government, industry, and academia—to work together for the betterment of the country and all its citizens. In addition to differing historical experiences, this view is a consequence of the region's collectivist values and holistic outlook that sees all parts of the greater whole (the nation) as being mutually connected and dependent and having a role to play.

What consequences does all this have for managing business in Asia? Societal orientation and the resultant considerations and obligations often preclude options that a company might otherwise wish to select—options that may be available to Western firms not under the aegis of such responsibilities. While common management practices in America and Europe, the following are two significant representative examples of options not as readily available to companies in many Asian markets due to the influence of the societal orientation of business.

Societal orientation and the resultant considerations and obligations often preclude options that a company might otherwise wish to select.

- Laying off employees in order to meet profit goals
- Downsizing to eliminate redundancies created by mergers, entering joint business projects with other firms, or ceasing certain business activities

Just how much stronger and prevalent is this broader—holistic—notion of societal obligation in Asian management? Singapore's parliament passed legislation in 1991 to codify in law the nation's traditional social values that made possible the country's economic success; it is referred to as the nation's "Shared Values," cited below. The very first of these official values states the priority of the nation's interests: "Nation before community and society above self."

Nothing gets lost in translation with this law—the interests of the nation and society take precedence over companies and individuals. This fundamental notion and also the high priority given to relationships are echoed in the legislation's section entitled "Consensus Not Conflict":

> *Singaporeans should participate in constructive discussion with sincerity and with the intention of upholding national interests. This value extends beyond state-civil relations: It also applies to disputes arising between unions and employers, communities, within families and in the commercial sphere.* —**(accessed April 12, 2021) Singapore's Shared Values can be accessed on the website of the Singapore National Library Board:** ***eresources.nlb.gov.sg/infopedia/articles/SIP_542_2004-12- 18***

A noteworthy example of this expectation that disputes between unions and employers should be engaged in constructively and with sincerity while upholding national interests is commonly seen in the manner bus strikes are conducted in the Japanese market.

I am always amazed to see that when bus drivers strike, they duly show up for work wearing their company uniforms and keep riding their bus's normal routes on their regular schedules. However, the drivers refuse to receive bus fares from passengers. In this way they uphold societal interest and stability by not inconveniencing the general public and all the places of employment the riders commute to. In addition to not inconveniencing society and harming the people's livelihood, this manner of striking results in greater financial pressure on the bus companies than a Western style employee walk out in the form of the expenses for the gasoline and vehicle wear and tear.

Mr. Loh Boon Chye, CEO of the Singapore Exchange, wrote in 2019 of the Asian notion of collective societal orientation, mutual interdependence, and holistic view and their importance to companies:

> *Finally, we are all accountable to each other. An ecosystem is sustainable only if its participants recognise their interdependence, and understand their respective roles. While it is not possible to completely align everyone's interests, it is possible to find a "centre of gravity" that everyone can gravitate towards. . . . I believe it starts with company boards.*—**Loh Boon Chye. "Taking a long-term view."** ***The Business Times.*** **July 28, 2019.** **(accessed April 29, 2021)** ***https://www.businesstimes.com.sg/opinion/taking-a-long-term-view***

Matsushita Konosuke, the founder and CEO of Japan's Panasonic Corporation (formerly known as the Matsushita Electric Co.), provided a compelling explanation of how fundamental the societal obligation of companies to employees and society at large is in Asian management as follows:

> *If the result of hard work is not black ink, and if it does not contribute to the prosperity of the country and the society nor to the enhancement of the standards of living of our employees, Matsushita Electric has no reason to exist. If it has no reason for existence, we should dissolve Matsushita Electric.* —**PHP Institute, Inc., *Matsushita Konosuke: His Life & Legacy* (Tokyo: PHP Institute, Inc., 1994), pp.34-35.**

Inamori Kazuo is founder and CEO of the Kyocera Corporation, one of Japan's most successful Fortune 50 companies and early world leader in industrial ceramics, and is regarded as the most prominent business leader in present day Japan. Not only does he echo the words of Matsushita, but he goes on to state that the very act of running a company—that is, *management itself*—is a service to society:

> *The pursuit of profit is the driving force behind business as well as many other human endeavors, and there is thus nothing wrong with wanting to make money. We should not pursue profit, however, for the benefit of ourselves alone. We need to "greedily" desire what is best for others and strive to promote the common [societal] good. If we do so, we too will benefit and the scope of our profit will greatly expand in the process.*
>
> *Running a company, for example, is in itself a service to others and to society.* —**Inamori Kazuo, *A Compass to Fulfillment: Passion and Spirituality in Life and Business* (New York: McGraw Hill, 2010), page 82.**

Chokwatana Boonsithi, the chairman of the Saha Group (Thailand's largest consumer products conglomerate comprised of nearly three hundred companies), likewise manages business with the view that companies should strive to benefit society as well as their bottom line: "There is no prosperity for oneself without others also benefiting."[8]

The following comment by Morita Akio, the co-founder and President of the Sony Corporation, also illustrates an enterprise's social responsibility and the different logic underlying Asian management:

> *I discovered very quickly that in Western countries, employers would get rid of some personnel when a recession seemed imminent. It was a shock to me, because in Japan we never do this, unless we are completely desperate. If the (company's) administration takes the risk and responsibility of hiring personnel, then it also assumes responsibility for giving them work. It's not the employee who is responsible for this agreement. Also, when there is a recession, why should the personnel suffer because of a decision made by the administration who gave them a job?*—(accessed May 25, 2021) ***http://www.quoteswise.com/akio-morita-quotes-2.html***

The practice of not laying off employees varies in degree among Asia's economies. In nations such as Singapore, Japan, and Korea, for example, large corporations avoid layoffs. While that

8 Chokwatana Boonsithi. "The Story of Thailand's Saha Group and its Chairman." Nikkei Asia. July 19, 2021 (accessed July 31, 2021) https://asia.nikkei.com/Spotlight/My-Personal-History/Boonsithi-Chokwatana/The-story-of-Thailand-s-Saha-Group-and-its-chairman-1.

was also the case in China, that has started to change recently. As that nation's economic growth has continued to slow down, major firms are matter-of-factly engaging in large-scale layoffs, plant closings, and asset liquidation in the same manner as their counterparts in the West do. Among non-state-owned companies, corporate interests can take precedence over societal well-being in China's current environment.

As we have seen, strong societal orientation is a fundamental factor in Asian management practices and can have both a direct and indirect influence on management strategies, options, tactics, and outcomes. In most Asian nations, however, companies also have the additional societal obligation to directly contribute to their government's economic development efforts. This obligation is greatest in the early stages of national economic development and then can diminish thereafter.

In Korea, for instance, the country's four major conglomerates—known as *chaebol* (재벌) in Korean—together are responsible for as much as eighty percent of the country's economy and, given their scale, have a far-reaching impact on the entire nation's well-being. It is common practice for these companies (Samsung, Hyundai, SK Group, and LG Group) to factor the economic development goals and objectives of their government into their management strategies and practices. One of Samsung's mottos succinctly states this nation-building, social obligation: "We do business for the sake of nation building!"

Toyota Sakichi, who provided the funding for his son Kiichiro to establish the Toyota Motor Corporation, echoes this societal orientation: "Build Cars! Build cars and serve your country." Article one of the company's official corporate policy states that mandate and even extends the geographic contribution Toyota should make: "While deeply cognizant of our mission in the automotive industry, we will actively contribute to economic and social development in Japan and worldwide."[9]

Singapore's IT giant, Grab Holdings, Inc., also extends this nation building commitment beyond its shores to the entire Southeast Asian region as noted in its corporate mission: "Drive Southeast Asia forward by creating economic empowerment for everyone."[10]

As a result of this societal obligation to actively contribute to the well-being of the entire nation, business and government commonly work in tandem. The result is that the objectives and policies of government and corporations commonly overlap and mutually reinforce each other.

As discussed, Asian companies working to achieve economic development goals set by their nation's governments and those governments providing special conditions to enable companies in that effort have been criticized in the West as business-government collusion. It has been seen as an obstacle preventing free and open markets from the vantage point of the West's form of capitalism. However, from the perspective of Asian management, businesses striving to meet government societal and economic objectives and benefiting from government policies to foster that is not collusion but rather collaboration that is a highly fundamental facet of a properly functioning society and economy. It is considered patriotic that Asian corporations

9 Satoshi Hino. *Inside The Mind of Toyota: Management Principles for Enduring Growth*. New York: Productivity Press, 2006, pages 2 and 52.

10 (Accessed May 2, 2021) https://www.grab.com/sg/our-story/.

support national goals and work to improve the social well-being of their country. It is expected, giving a broader meaning to the phrase good corporate citizen than found in the West. It also highlights the divergent logic, goals, and priorities that guide Asian management.

Figure 3: Degree of Influence of Societal Orientation on Management

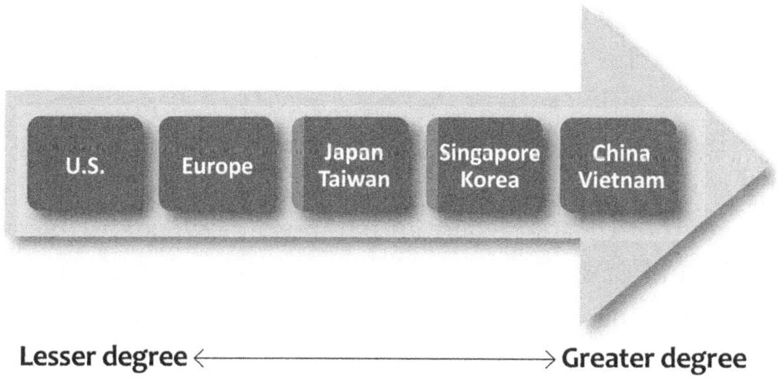

Source: Robert Charles Azar, 2021

While the societal obligation to contribute to their government's economic directions is prevalent in Asia, the degree to which governments and society need their companies to align corporate and government plans and actions varies as seen in Figure 3. History has shown that in early stages of developing a modern economy, government-business cooperation is its strongest because the need for it is greatest at that time. As each country progresses from being a developing economy to a developed nation, the need and extent of this cooperation diminishes. This is seen in the economic development of China, Japan, Korea, Taiwan, Singapore, Thailand, Indonesia, Malaysia, and Vietnam.

This influence of government on a country's economy and corporations is greatest in Asian countries with state-run economies, such as China and Vietnam. In those markets, large percentages of major corporations are state owned and run (especially in the early stages of the nation building a modern economy), and they are obliged to follow the five- and ten-year economic development plans that their country's governments formulate. Chinese firms account for one hundred and nine companies among the Fortune 500 Global corporations. Of those, eighty-five percent are government owned. State-owned enterprises (SOEs) produce forty percent of the nation's total GDP.[11]

In China, the central government keeps members of the ruling communist party on the board of directors of major corporations (both state-owned and non-state-owned) to provide oversight and maintain direct influence on the operations of the country's leading companies. While this political corporate governance coexists with China's legal corporate governance, it is not uncommon for the former to exert a dominant influence.[12]

The COVID-19 pandemic provides numerous examples in China of the obligation of companies to work for the overall benefit of society. For example, in March 2020, President Xi Jinping ordered state-owned enterprises to step up "unconditionally and at any cost" deal with this national emergency. One of the results was that state-owned enterprises built a 1,000-bed hospital and a 1,600-bed facility in just ten days. While many *private manufacturers* struggled to restore production, more than 95 percent of some 20,000 *government-controlled manufacturers* produced masks, medicines, steel, heavy machinery, and

11 World Economic Forum. Explained, the role of China's state-owned companies. May 7, 2019. (accessed June 14, 2021) https://www.weforum.org/agenda/2019/05/why-chinas-state-owned-companies-still-have-a-key-role-to-play/

12 Bruce Aronson and Joongi Kim, editors. *Corporate Governance in Asia: A Comparative Approach*. Cambridge, United Kingdom: Cambridge University Press, 2019. Page 261.

other products needed in responding to COVID-19—providing corporate revenues and keeping workers on the job. As one regulator at the State-Owned Assets Supervision and Administration Commission (SASAC), the agency that regulates state-owned enterprises, described it:

> *It's like in a battlefield, and state-owned enterprises are the ones who can act fast and decisively.* —**China's Coronavirus Response Toughens State Control and Weakens the Private Market.** ***Wall Street Journal*** **3/18/20.**—(accessed August 1, 2021) ***https://www.wsj.com/articles/chinas-coronavirus-response-toughens-state-control-and-weakens-the-private-market-11584540534***

In conclusion, societal orientation and obligation of companies is a fundamental facet of Asian management and plays a much greater role in the region than in the West. International executives need to factor that into managing their business operations and relationships in those markets. As noted, divergent societal expectations can result in an Asian partner not being able to utilize management practices that Western executives routinely employ and take for granted. Consequently, it is highly recommended that Western companies fully discuss and confirm early in their discussions with potential Asian partners the viability of management strategies, plans, and expected execution options in light of these differences.

In addition to precluding management practices and options that Western executives are accustomed to, societal orientation can require international companies to change their customary business model and operations. This facet of managing in Asia is further discussed in the company case studies in chapter seven.

IV. COMPANY AS SOCIETY

We have seen that in many Asian markets, corporations are reluctant to lay off workers as a consequence of their societal orientation and obligations. Another reason management views layoffs negatively is that they are mindful that the accumulated experience, loyalty, and industry relationships of their employees bring significant value to a company in several ways. The following are representative examples of this value:

- Long-term employees provide the firm with decades of firsthand, in-house expertise.
- Employees are willing to work longer hours beyond the official end of their work day.
- Greater job security results in employees working with greater dedication and focus.
- Employment longevity fosters heightened levels of collaboration and synergies within the company, avoiding the silo effect found in other regions of the world whereby departments operate with less communication and coordination with each other or with outright rivalry.

There also is another reason why Asian companies lay off workers to a lesser degree than in the West. And it has nothing to do with the interests of the company, but rather points to the significance that a company has to all its members. Going beyond simply providing a product or service and employment, a company is often thought of as a worker's community or mini society, a place where needs normally fulfilled by society at large can be met, to varying degrees, within the company.

- The company becomes a central part of the workers' social lives as employees typically socialize with co-workers during lunch, after business hours, and on weekends.

- Larger companies provide housing cost savings for employees by renting them housing in company-owned buildings or dormitories for free or far below market prices.

- Larger firms provide complimentary day care for the children of employees, giving employees not only the financial benefit but also the peace of mind of knowing their children are well taken care while they spend long hours at work.

- In addition to making a social network there, it is not uncommon for workers to look for and find their spouses in their workplace.

- Employees in more traditionally oriented companies hesitate to take vacations even though they have plenty of vacation time accumulated. As a result, companies often arrange and even pay for company vacations where all employees go as a group. In this way, management thanks all the employees for their efforts on behalf of the firm while not singling out individual workers. This arrangement provides several benefits:

- Corporate trips build company morale.
- Company vacations enhance employee loyalty.
- Corporate junkets further strengthen the social and work bonds among workers.
- Company getaways promote group solidarity within the company, reinforcing the collectivist dynamics that underpin Asian management practices.

When comparing the words for "company" and "society" in China, Japan, Korea, and Taiwan, I was amazed to discover that the similarity between company and society can also be seen linguistically in all four countries. The word for company is 会社, and the word for society is 社会. Both words are written with the same two characters, just in reverse order. In other words, company = society (会社 = 社会) and society = company (社会 = 会社). Whenever I have mentioned this to friends and colleagues in Asia over the years, they are surprised saying that, while they never consciously made the connection between the characters for company and society being the same, the implication certainly is true.

The company functioning as a self-contained community or mini society is indicative of the holistic outlook found in Asian business culture. From management's vantage, corporations taking a holistic view toward their employees enables a workforce to be more content, loyal, stable, and motivated. This allows staff to work without distractions and at higher levels of flexibility, productivity, and efficiency. As Prime Minister Lee Kuan Yew, the founder and first Prime Minister of modern Singapore, stated:

"Invest in your staff, they are your business." —**The Finder.**—(accessed May 1, 2021) ***https://www.thefinder.com.sg/healthy-living/the-best-quotes-from-mr-lee-kuan-yew-for-business-leaders/?agallery=45025&aslide=8***

It is factors such as these that underlie the strong sense of employee-company commitment to one's work and company that can be found in Asian firms. Employee dedication to their company and work, however, is not a one way affair; instead, it is a two way street through which a company earns employee commitment by demonstrating commitment to its workers. One common way Asian companies do so is through the social aid they provide their employees. In addition to the popular forms of social aid mentioned above, companies may offer the following:

- Healthcare benefits
- Pension programs
- Financial gift upon birth of children
- Discounted housing
- Employee-use only company vacation properties
- Company owned restaurants offering discounted dining
- Annual physical health checkups
- Free fitness center access

The prevalence of employee commitment varies across Asia, typically more commonplace in Japan, Korea, Taiwan, and Vietnam and less so in China where workers are more often motivated by the desire to advance one's career and earn a better living as is common in the West. Employee attitudes across the region also vary depending on age, with younger workers often less influenced by the region's traditional values in general and employee outlooks in particular.

It is noteworthy that employee commitment to one's company being weaker in China than in Japan can be seen linguistically in the word for "employee" in the languages of both nations. In China, employee is written as 员工 (*yuangong*) which means "member of work"; it means to be a participant in the work but does not infer belonging to the firm. In Japan, employee is written as 社員 (*shain*) which means "member of the company" and, accordingly, includes the meaning of belonging to the firm.

Chapter 2

MANAGING COMPANIES: *Key Practices*

You can be totally rational with a machine. But if you work with people, sometimes logic often has to take a backseat to understanding. —**Morita Akio**

Different people have to be managed differently.— **Dr. Peter Drucker**

I. COLLECTIVIST MANAGEMENT

It was the day of very important follow-up meetings between the management team of my San Francisco-based client and senior executives of the Japanese corporation I had recommended to be their partner in that market. Our initial meeting in Tokyo twelve days earlier had gone very well, and the subsequent dialogue had all parties involved optimistic regarding the merits of working together.

The Japanese executives were arriving to visit the company in San Francisco for a second round of lengthy face-to-face discussions. I met them at the airport and drove them to my client company's corporate headquarters, where guest parking was in front of the main entrance. As I was parking in the visitor's parking spaces near the building's main entrance, one of the executives pointed to a sign at the parking space closest to the front door. With great surprise he stated in Japanese, "What is that?" The sign read: "Reserved for salesman of the month." After I translated the message into Japanese for the rest of the executives, all of them were amazed. One of them articulated their surprise by commenting: "That would be inconceivable in Japan."

He is right. It is rare in many Asian markets that an individual would be singled out for anything, let alone be given recognition as prominent as their own parking spot right in front of the main entrance to the company's corporate headquarters. As discussed, while Western societies are strongly individual-oriented, Asian societies are just as strongly group-oriented—another aspect of the different approaches, rationales, and logic utilized in both regions.

In the West, management and human resource practices focus on the individual and are geared toward developing, coordinating, and motivating individuals. In Asian markets, the focus is on developing, coordinating, and motivating teams or departments. This is illustrative of how Asia's indigenous management practices are collectivist in nature, aiming at enhancing the cohesiveness, loyalty, and performance of the entire group.

For example, in the event of a sales competition in American and European companies, individual salespeople typically compete with each other. The winners are individuals—the individual in first place gets, for instance, the salesman of the month parking spot or a paid vacation. In Asian companies, sales competitions are between groups—sales team A versus sales team B or the Shenzhen sales team versus the Shanghai sales team. The winning team is congratulated as a group for their superior performance. Generally speaking, individuals are not singled out.

A case in point, I had just started working with an American client as their consultant to oversee their business in Asia. On my first visit to their Seoul offices, I was informed the new American manager there had just tried to give an award to the top performing salesman the previous month, and it was disastrous. The manager had the salesman stand up during a sales meeting to be recognized and to receive a round of applause. The salesman was utterly mortified. His co-workers were at a loss in this alien situation. The manager, seeing that this management practice he had used so successfully for years in the States did not work in a major Asian market, realized that he had a problem. Instead of resulting in a stronger relationship with the sales team he was sent to manage, he had alienated himself from them. He was never able to get the relationship back on track, and the performance of the company's most able salesperson was never the same for the remainder of that American executive's stay in Korea. Simply put, domestic management practices often do not travel well due to the differing management fundamentals that define each international market.

Domestic management practices often do not travel well due to the differing management fundamentals that define each international market.

Dr. Peter Drucker understood the benefits of group-oriented management and leadership in business. Drucker wrote:

> *The leaders who work most effectively, it seems to me, never say "I." And that's not because they have trained themselves not to say "I." They don't think "I." They think "we"; they think "team." They understand their job to be to make the team function. They accept responsibility and don't sidestep it, but "we" gets the credit. This is what creates trust, what enables you to get the task done.*—**(accessed May 20, 2021) https://www.goodreads.com/author/quotes/12008.Peter_F_Drucker, page 1.**

What are the social dynamics that underlie Asia's collectivist management? It is part of the holistic approach, rationale, and logic fundamental to Asian cultures and business practices that sees all parties as interconnected and mutually dependent. One feature of this collectivist management is that one does not want to stand out, be singled out, or be different.

In Asia, the social and cultural importance of not standing out or not being different is most pronounced in Japan, where, for example, the word for different in the Japanese language is *chigau* (違う), which means not only "to be different" but also "to be wrong." By definition, what is different is, quite literally, also considered to be wrong. Conversely, if you want to be correct, you need to be the same, to blend in, not draw attention to oneself—in other words, to act in a group-oriented manner.

While collectivism with its group orientation is commonplace throughout the Asian region, its prevalence in management practices varies country to country, as illustrated in the following figure.

Figure 4: Degree of Collectivism in Corporate Management

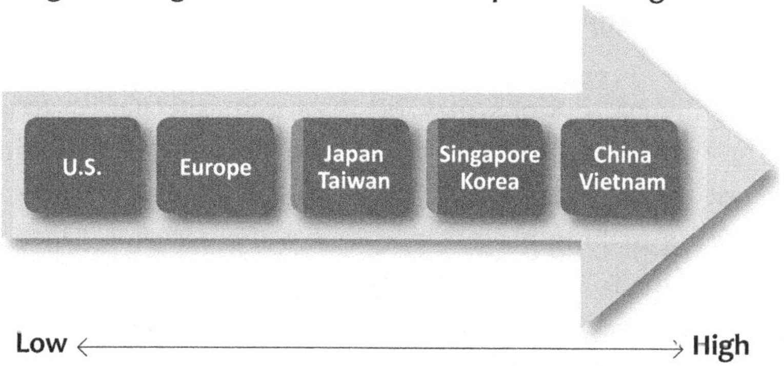

Source: Robert Charles Azar, 2021

When managing in Asia, it is important for international executives to keep in mind the collectivist dynamics in those markets. Management techniques that focus on the individual can end up being counterproductive. At a minimum, they make all parties involved feel awkward and inhibit effective business collaboration. In the worst case, they can alienate the parties involved, limit progress, and negatively impact company growth and profitability.

Another area where Western executives experience the impact of collectivist management early on is corporate decision-making. Let's take a look at that facet of management next.

II. DECISION-MAKING

Management decision-making is typically conducted in a top-down fashion in Western markets. The senior most person calls the shots and what is decided is communicated to those affected by it for implementation. It is not uncommon for those impacted by those decisions to hear about them for the first time after the decision has already been made, and in some cases, only at the time of implementation.

Different options may be discussed; alternative actions may be recommended by other participants in the discussions; however, in the end, it is the senior most executive involved in the decision-making process who makes the decision. Once the decision is made, it is passed down to all relevant parties in the company for execution. In this way, decision-making takes place at the top of the department or organization and flows down to the rank and file in a top-down manner.

In Asian nations, international executives experience two major types of decision-making. First, countries such as China and Thailand also utilize a top-down method of decision-making similar to the West. Second, in Japan, Korea, Singapore, Taiwan, Indonesia, and Vietnam, a quite different type of decision-making is used, namely group-oriented decision-making.

In contrast to top-down decision-making, group decision-making is a very involved, meticulous, and time-consuming method involving not only more participants but also a bottom-up process. All parties involved with the decision and its ramifications are included in the discussions from the very beginning and in every step throughout the entire decision-making process. Let's examine how this typically works.

A proposal will be circulated to all those departments or parties who will be affected as well as those who should be aware of the matter to be decided, such as senior executives. Each party will thoroughly review the proposal, closely looking at three fundamental considerations:

- **Proposal's effectiveness:** Is the proposal the best way to achieve its stated objective and intended purpose from the perspective of each individual stakeholder? If not, ways to maximize the proposal's effectiveness and efficiencies are formulated and added by each party concerned.

- **Proposal's requirements:** What will each department need to do to carry out the proposal? Each department will identify, define, and analyze the specifics and calculate the requisite costs as it considers the proposal.

- **Proposal's impact:** How will the proposal impact each individual party? What will be the impact on productivity rates, quality control, cost, workload, employee morale, sales, the company's competitive standing in the market, and the firm's social standing? Each department will offer ways to avoid, or at least minimize, negative consequences and also offer ways to maximize the proposal's benefits. After that, each individual party will examine how the proposal will impact their dealings with other departments within their company as well as with stakeholders outside of the firm such as suppliers, vendors, and customers.

After concluding this initial and time-consuming review of the proposal, each participating party will add the results of their review to the proposal. The revised proposal document will then be circulated again to all groups involved. Each group goes through subsequent reviews of the document as the additions of all the other groups are added, each time again checking the proposal's requirements, effectiveness, and impact. Once all parties have reviewed and revised the proposal to best take into consideration their situation, the content of the proposal becomes finalized. The head of each department involved in this process stamps the seal of his department on it (literally), signifying that the department has officially approved the proposal's content. The proposal must be approved by each and every department involved for the decision to be adopted.

Decision-making thus requires all departments to work together to consider and ensure that the needs and interests of each and every department involved are addressed. This is consistent with the collectivist management view that all parties are mutually connected and interdependent. Just as this internal decision-making process requires allowing for the business interests of the other departments *within a company*, decision-making *between business partners* likewise involves taking into account the business interests of all the companies involved. Accordingly, taking into account the interests of other involved parties applies both to *intra-company* as well as *inter-company* decision-making. This decision-making dynamic is based upon the holistic approach, rationale, and logic governing the region's indigenous management practices.

This method of group decision-making is used throughout much of the region and to the greatest degree in the Japanese market, where it is referred to as *ringi* (稟議). The following flow chart illustrates this collectivist decision-making process.

As one can easily imagine, this process is quite tedious

Figure 5: Japanese Ringi (稟議) Method of Group Decision-Making

Decision-Making Steps	Upper Management	Middle Management	Lower Management and Staff
Step 1: Potential issues identified	Issues reviewed	Potential issues identified	Potential issues identified
Step 2: Issues selected	Issues selected and announced	Directive to find solution received	
Step 3: Solutions identified		Jointly identify possible solutions	
Step 4: Solutions vetted and finalized		Analyze and recommend solution options	
Step 5: Internal decision-making	Solution selected	**Inter**department consensus	**Intra**department consensus
Step 6: Solution authorized and announced	Solution mandated	Solution decision received	Solution decision received
Step 7: Solution execution		Solution decision implemented	

Source: Robert Charles Azar, 2021

and time consuming. It can be even more slow moving when consensus is required for major items. However, the advantages of this method of group decision-making often outweigh the disadvantages.

Because each group or department of the company affected by a proposal is continuously involved in the decision-making process from beginning to end, they are all fully knowledgeable about the proposal contents when it is time for implementation. They all are keenly aware of what the proposal will require of them, how it will impact them, and what practical steps they will need to take to prepare for and execute it. As a result, they are fully informed and ready to implement the proposal as soon as the decision is finalized.

Furthermore, since all the relevant parties include their recommendations in the decision and give it their approval, they have shared ownership and responsibility regarding the outcome of the decision. Consequently, once it is time to implement the decision, each participating party has a vested interest in making sure the decision is implemented as successfully as possible. As a result, another benefit of Asian collectivist decision-making is that resistance to implementing new decisions or the changes they necessitate is far less common than in the West.

In contrast, in a top-down decision-making process, the affected parties often start to examine what is required of them, how it will impact them, and what changes and costs will be required only *after* the decision has been made and announced. This often causes a delay between the time a decision is announced and when it can be implemented. In addition, as the affected parties were not involved in the decision, there are occasions when they resist implementing the decision because of potential detrimental effects. Even worse, new initiatives and their requisite changes may be sabotaged or outright ignored by managers who deem them not in the best interest of their department or their own personal career.

Western executives experience a negative consequence of Asia's group decision-making practice during their initial negotiations. Asian executives are often not in a position to make decisions on the spot during negotiation sessions. There must be time for conferring with all the parties involved. This is one of the reasons why the pace of negotiations is slower and the overall time span for negotiations is considerably longer in Asia than in the West.

III. VERTICAL AND HORIZONTAL ALIGNMENT OF MANAGEMENT

Another benefit of collectivist management and decision-making that I experienced working in Asian markets is the greater degree of alignment or enrollment of departments, management, and rank and file employees within companies regarding corporate decisions and actions. Management alignment takes place in two ways: vertical and horizontal.

Vertical management alignment occurs when the various levels of management and rank-and-file employees within one department are enrolled in a decision. Horizontal management alignment takes place when the management of the company's numerous departments are enrolled.

> Collectivist management and decision-making results in a greater degree of alignment of departments, management, and rank and file employees within companies.

As the decision-making flow chart in Figure 5 illustrates, all levels of management as well as workers within each department participate in, agree to, and commit to company decisions. Consequently, each department is vertically aligned or on board with decisions to a degree less common in the West. In addition, as all departments horizontally confer and cooperate with each other in the decision-making process, they are horizontally aligned with each other through their mutual enrollment in agreed upon strategies and plans. In this way, departments in large corporations utilizing collectivist decision-making typically experience a greater degree of vertical and horizontal alignment compared to firms in other regions. The vertical and horizontal alignments of management are illustrated in the following figure.

Figure 6: Vertical and Horizontal Alignment of Management

Management Department	Sales Department	R&D Department	Production Department	Finance Department	HR Department
C-Suite Executives	C-Suite Executives	C-Suite Executives	C-Suite Executives	C-Suite Executives	C-Suite Executives
Senior Executives	Senior Executives	Senior Executives	Senior Executives	Senior Executives	Senior Executives
Middle Management	Middle Management	Middle Management	Middle Management	Middle Management	Middle Management
Lower Management	Lower Management	Lower Management	Lower Management	Lower Management	Lower Management
Non-Management Workers	Non-Management Workers	Non-Management Workers	Non-Management Workers	Non-Management Workers	Non-Management Workers

Vertical alignment within each department

Horizontal alignment across departments

Source: Robert Charles Azar, 2021

Having its departments and their various levels of employees in agreement on and committed to common decisions allows an Asian corporation to apply all its resources and full strength to management initiatives to a degree often greater than in other markets. This is the result of—and also reinforces—the holistic nature of Asian management as the interests of all involved stakeholders are duly taken into account. In addition, it enables companies to more effectively engage in long-term management as the entire organization is enrolled, committed, and prepared to carry out its objectives for the long haul. This holistic dynamic of Asian management is what enables the region's ubiquitous five- and ten-year plans to be achievable—as opposed to merely aspirational—commitments for advancing business and government interests.

It is noteworthy that while collectivist decision-making is common throughout the region, there is an interesting difference among China, Japan, Korea, Taiwan, and Vietnam. Large corporations in all these markets will have management proposals circulate widely among departments. In Japan and Taiwan, the aim is to have all parties affected by decisions participate in order to improve proposals, be thoroughly prepared for implementing them, and be fully committed to them. In China, Korea, and Vietnam, however, group decision-making can also be utilized to allow management to spread accountability to multiple departments in the event of poor results.

As noted, indigenous Asian decision-making requires a greater amount of time, is based on a different management rationale, and involves different methods. Western executives need to fully prepare for these fundamental differences when managing their operations with business partners and their own locally staffed operations in the region.

IV. CHANGE, RISK, AND PROBLEM SOLVING

Another challenge international executives commonly find in Asian markets as a result of differing management fundamentals is the different approach to change, risk, and problem solving.

A. CHANGE AND RISK

Asia is often referred to as a region of paradox. While many of its countries have all the trappings of ultramodern, technologically advanced, industrialized nations, they also hold on to practices and norms that are centuries old. This paradox can also be found in attitudes toward change and risk.

On the one hand, progress, innovation, and improvement receive high priority in business throughout Asia and are aggressively pursued. For instance, the world-famous practice of *kaizen* (continual improvement) and just in time inventory, fundamental management practices that have been adopted worldwide as best business practices, originated in Japan. At the same time, however, Asian societies can simultaneously possess an aversion to change that disrupts the status quo. There can also be a wariness regarding the risks inherent in change. These impact Asian management practices and affect how companies operate.

In the West, comparatively speaking, we are more receptive to change and tolerant of risk. This is especially true in the States where we see both as an opportunity to welcome in what is new, improve a product or technology, and execute operations better. Furthermore, change is central to America's entrepreneurial culture where it is deliberately sought out and exploited. In his book *Innovation and Entrepreneurship: Practice and Principles*, Dr. Peter Drucker noted: "The entrepreneur always searches for change, responds to it, and exploits it as an opportunity." In short, change has long been a major driver of entrepreneurialism and success in business.

Failure is likewise viewed differently. In Asia, it is seen as a consequence of insufficient planning, ineffective execution, or dysfunction in business relationships—and it causes one to lose face. In contrast, failure in the U.S. is often viewed as an opportunity to learn how to do it better next time. As two major figures in the development of American industry famously put it:

"I have not failed. I've just found 10,000 ways that won't work."—**Thomas Edison**

"Failure is only the opportunity to begin again, only this time more wisely." —**Henry Ford**

The history of Asian nations goes back thousands of years, and there is considerable historical momentum as well as social and cultural causes behind the status quo and the established way of doing things. As we discussed in Asian decision-making, reaching agreement on what is the status quo took an inordinate amount of time and effort, resulting in resistance to changing it. As noted, standing out or being different also has traditionally not been viewed favorably.

In America, with a comparatively very short history and great population diversity, the historical momentum of cultural traditions does not carry the same force. We do not feel as bound by established practices of the past and, instead, are more focused on the possibilities of the future. Change is the gateway to those possibilities. Indeed, America is the home of the concept of finding breakthrough technologies and products as well as industry disrupters. With a shorter history, the U.S. has always looked to the new ways of the future as opposed to the status quo.

By way of contrast, in Asian societies there is an established and proper protocol for most things. This provides clarity and certainty and makes clear how everyone can act in a way that is proper and respectful. The status quo is to be respected and maintained. An abrupt or major change will require time for a new group consensus to be reached and, based on that, to put in place a new status quo. As a consequence, change is often met with resistance. In Japan, for example, one of the words for change (*dou* 動) also means confusion. Also, the disruption that change brings is referred to not as uncertainty but as *konran* (混乱), which means confusion, disorder, chaos, and mayhem.

Having an aversion to sudden change goes hand in hand with not proactively seeking what is different. This less welcoming view of change and failure is one of the reasons that entrepreneurship has traditionally not been prevalent in Asia to the degree it is in non-collectivist societies such as the U.S. and other Western markets.

B. PROBLEM SOLVING: PROCESS OVER PURPOSE

The emphasis on knowing and following established procedures and the prescribed way of doing things results in giving great priority to process when striving for solutions or improvements. The way to attain the right results is to ensure that the process and procedures are right. For example, the title of the first of the Toyota Motor Corporation's fourteen principles—the bible of Toyota's management practices—delineates this in the following manner: *"The Right Process Will Produce the Right Results."*[13]

The current honorary Chairman of Toyota Motor Corporation, Cho Fujio, went so far as to state that process is more important than the caliber of employees in determining a firm's success when he discussed the priority of process:

> *We get brilliant results from average people managing brilliant processes—while our competitors get average*

13 Jeffrey K. Liker, *The Toyota Way: 14 Management Principles from the World's Greatest Manufacturer*. New York:McGraw-Hill, 2004. Page 87.

> *or worse results from brilliant people managing broken processes.*—(accessed March 16, 2021) ***https://www.azquotes.com/author/22307-Fujio_Cho***

More than analyzing a situation from a conceptional perspective in seeking an improvement or solution, workers are encouraged to find them through direct action. This hands-on, experiential approach is the basis of *kaizen* (continual improvement) that has spread from its beginnings in Japan to being adopted throughout the world. As Mr. Cho indicated:

> *We place the highest value on actual implementation and taking action. There are many things one doesn't understand and therefore, we ask them why don't you just go ahead and take action, try to do something? . . . So by constant improvement, or, should I say, the improvement based upon action, one can rise to the higher level of practice and knowledge.*—(accessed March 16, 2021) ***https://www.azquotes.com/author/22307-Fujio_Cho***

This emphasis of precedence and procedure over purpose is another example of the different approach, rationale, and logic of the region. It can be extremely frustrating to Western executives who are inclined to conceptualize a situation, seek solutions, use linear logic, and strive for quick implementation.

The basis for this approach is in part the Confucian tenet that the prescribed way to do something is the proper way to do it, and, therefore, the way it should be done. Engaging in actions in the prescribed manner (that is, in accordance with established procedure) is the very essence of Confucianism's central principle of following established norms and ritual propriety (*li* 礼 in Chinese).

> This emphasis of precedence and procedure over purpose is an example of the different logic of the region.

Furthermore, this outlook is consistent with the holistic approach of Asian management. It is in looking at the total *process* that one can see all the parts of the whole situation, their relationship with each other, how they function together, and how they depend on each other. The challenge this approach can present to Western executives is that following proper procedure can be more important than how to achieve the procedure's purpose or do it better.

International executives will experience instances when the purpose-focused and conceptual approach of the West finds solutions or achieves results more directly, yet quickly implementing that solution can be met with resistance both to altering established procedure (process) and the requirements of the change. As a former European client expressed it: "I continue to be amazed at how things are done in this country. To have such a past for production efficiencies it does indeed boggle the mind when it comes to application of what we Western thinkers refer to as common sense. The challenges continue to mount, but I believe I am recognizing a common denominator in process."

In addition to the factors above, there are several other social dynamics that can result in resistance to change in Asia:

- Respect for seniors requires younger employees to be deferential to those with seniority, even when from an objective perspective, the younger employee has the better idea.

- It is not polite to disagree.
- Maintaining the status quo is central to collectivist dynamics, including productive relationships.
- Upholding the status quo is necessary for operations to proceed smoothly and for organizations to be run effectively.

How, then, does one achieve change in a status quo environment? In what manner is change addressed in Asia? As is so often true in much of the region, there is a proper time and place for everything. In the context of business, the culturally accepted opportunity and venue to discuss change and improvement is the review or evaluation meeting. Employees discuss at great length how to do things better—how to do them more efficiently, more cost effectively, more successfully. Employees are encouraged to speak freely and openly. The customary cultural dynamics of not disagreeing and of being deferential to those more senior are relaxed in the review meeting. It is noteworthy that the three characters of the word for review meeting in the Japanese language (*hansei-kai* 反省会) mean "anti-," "save or conserve," and "meeting," clearly indicating that the purpose of the review meeting is to be against conserving established procedure, process, and protocols.

In the West, we utilize brainstorming sessions to achieve the same goals of the review meeting. The difference between the two is that review meetings typically are held with much greater frequency and last longer. For example, they can be held at the end of every shift, the end of every production cycle, the end of every day, week, month, quarter, and year, or even all these. They can last a few hours or a few days. I experienced on numerous occasions attending review meetings that lasted several days, the longest being three-and-a-half days of early morning to late at night discussions.

How can international executives best manage their business interests in Asian markets on a day-to-day basis in light of this differing attitude toward change, risk, and problem solving?

First, utilizing the review meeting is imperative. It is the best opportunity to find out what issues are affecting your workers and your business. It is the best place to constructively discuss the options for best navigating those issues. Review meetings may produce suggestions that enhance your intended change or are superior to it. These meetings can be so lengthy that Western executives find them to be tedious and nerve-racking to attend. However, it is well worth it in the end to conduct them regularly.

Second, keeping in mind that decision-making is done as a group, meet with appropriate managers who will be involved with the decision-making and implementation ahead of time to plant seeds for the upcoming change. The goal is to inform them about what may be involved and get them on board before the need for change is officially announced in the company. This practice of advanced, behind-the-scenes stage setting is a common method for laying the groundwork for change, managing risk, and implementing new initiatives. In Japan, this practice has been raised to the status of an art form referred to as *nemawashi* (根回し).

Third, in addition to those who will participate in

decision-making, whenever possible include those who will be impacted by a change or new initiative. This will make acceptance and implementation of the change smoother and more widespread throughout your company or joint business project. It could also lead to alternative options that are more effective than what you originally planned to implement—one of the key benefits of the group method of decision-making as discussed above.

Sometimes, for one reason or another, it is not possible to use any of these methods. I developed three alternative practices that have served my clients well over the years on both the executive as well as day-to-day management levels:

- When at all possible, *avoid abruptly announcing that changes are to take effect immediately*. An effective way to introduce change is to inform your Asian colleagues, subordinates, and partners ahead of time of anticipated changes. In the event that the details of the change are not finalized or are still unknown, informing them that at this point an unspecified change is expected goes a long way to preparing them for change when more details become available. It removes the element of surprise and alerts them so they are now prepared to expect changes to the status quo. It also is consistent with and reinforces the inclusive nature of Asia's collectivist management.

  Avoiding sudden change reduces Asian concern that the change is a response to an unanticipated problem with your product or business, or, even worse, that the alterations are an afterthought on your part, something you overlooked previously and only now realized needed to be included.

By providing advance notice before the implementation date, you give Asian colleagues the time they need to build consensus strategies among themselves regarding how best to incorporate the change.

- *Refer to change as an advancement or benefit.* Rather than calling it change, refer to it by the positive benefit(s) that will result. If the change is in the area of the timeliness of customer service, for example, then refer to it as "an even quicker response time." If the change refers to major product functions or features, then identify the change as "the next generation" of your product. Framing change as the positive benefit it will produce translates well in the context of Asian management practices by eliminating the notion that confusion will result from change.

- *Show how the changes will result in your product or business operations being more in line with "best global business practices."* Being on the cutting edge and up to date with leading international business norms resonates well as a reason for initiating change or taking risk. In addition, since you are positioning the alterations as being in line with best *global* business practices, and not with American or European business ways of doing things, the changes become more palatable for your Asian colleagues. You are not asking them to give up their indigenous ways and replace them with Western practices since global practices are nationality neutral.

These approaches to introducing and managing change and risk are more acceptable to your Asian partners, will help enable smooth and comprehensive implementation, and will reduce the occurrence of resistance.

I have often heard Western business executives downplay the importance of acknowledging and dealing with cultural differences, failing to recognize the impact they can have. Cultural differences are often considered fluff, third tier considerations that have little bearing on a company's business results. However, management and human resource approaches that lack a group focus typically exacerbate, rather than reduce, the inherent and ever-present challenges from culture-based differences in business practices between Westerners and Asians working in the same organization or collaborating on a joint project. As a direct result, worker morale, motivation, focus, and commitment are adversely affected. The net-net result is diminished sales performance and bottom-line profitability as an immediate result of culture-based differences in management practices.

Despite their role and impact being fundamental and far-reaching, culture-based differences in management fundamentals are typically a major overlooked causal factor in international business performance.

Culture-based differences in management fundamentals are typically a major overlooked causal factor in international business performance.

They are rarely factored into analysis of a company's business results to the degree warranted, all to the detriment of Western firms.

Chapter 3

MANAGING BUSINESS PARTNERS

Robert Lutz, former Vice-Chairman of Chrysler and key figure in the Daimler-Chrysler merger, said, "There was a remarkable meeting of the minds at the senior management level. They look like us, they talk like us, they're focused on the same things, and their command of English is impeccable. There was definitely no culture clash there."[14]

Unfortunately, his statement that "there was definitely no culture clash" between the two companies proved disastrously mistaken. Within just two years, the merger between these two veteran global corporations fell apart and was dissolved. Differences in management fundamentals was one of the primary

14 Interview with Robert Lutz, Former Vice-Chairman, Chrysler Corp. Cited in Tuck School of Business at Dartmouth, The DaimlerChrysler Merger. (accessed July 24, 2020) https://docplayer.net/11234758-The-daimlerchrysler-merger.html.

causes. The submerged part of the management practice iceberg mentioned in this book's Introduction sank another major international business venture—this time between two proven titans of business with a combined one hundred and sixty years of business experience between them at that time.

Note this clash in management practices was between two Western companies with shared social, political, economic, cultural, historical, and religious values. From this perspective, think how much greater the clash in management fundamentals is between a Western and an Asian firm with profoundly different social, political, economic, cultural, historical, and religious values.

The central role of relationship in business is one of the primary areas where the divergent management practices of Asia and the West are incongruous. Let's begin this chapter discussing the key role of relationship in traditional Asian business.

I. CENTRALITY OF RELATIONSHIP

In comparing the West and Asia, so many of the fundamental differences in management practices and the dynamics that underpin them stem from the central role of relationship. It impacts numerous facets of indigenous Asian management including these:

1. Approach to management
2. Purpose of management
3. Corporate objectives
4. Investment priorities

5. Sales goals
6. Meaning of value creation
7. Dynamics governing management
8. Degree of importance given to the interests of business partners and employees
9. Protocols informing partner relationships and interactions
10. Hiring, developing, and promoting of employees
11. Method of presenting business objectives
12. Timing for presenting one's corporate interests
13. Dealing with differences in corporate positions
14. Depth of information requested and disclosed
15. Degree of compromising necessary in business relationships
16. Conflict resolution
17. Pace of discussions and business plan implementation
18. Communication dynamics
19. Length of meetings
20. Who participates in projects and meetings
21. Seating arrangements
22. Venue of business discussions
23. Customer satisfaction
24. Stakeholder obligations
25. Preference for raising capital through debt versus equities

Given the paramount significance of relationship in Asian business in general and management practices in particular, a good place to start is to understand what "relationship" actually means in Asia. This is true for both *inter*-party management relating to business partners and customers and *intra*-party management of a corporation's departments and employees.

A. DIVERGENT MEANINGS OF RELATIONSHIP

In Western business, when we say two companies have a relationship, it generally means, excluding any ownership ties, that the two companies have conducted business together. It is not necessary to have a relationship in order to establish business collaboration. Instead, two companies conduct business together and then a relationship follows. A relationship is typically the result of engaging in business together. In short, in the West, business *collaboration precedes relationship*. Equally important, *relationship is the result of collaboration.*

The meaning of relationship throughout Asia varies significantly in both nuance and substance from market to market.

This is quite different from relationship in Asian business. Actually, it is the exact opposite. Generally speaking, having a relationship is a prerequisite in order for companies to begin to work together. Consequently, while collaboration precedes relationship in the West, in Asia *relationship precedes collaboration.* Furthermore, *relationship enables companies to conduct business together* in Asia; relationship is not the result of collaboration as is the case in the West.

What then does relationship mean in Asia? On its most basic level, relationship means having a comfort level and familiarity with the other party. That meaning is commonplace in most of Asia and serves as a good baseline definition. However, the meaning of relationship throughout Asia varies significantly in both nuance and substance from market to market. Let's take a closer look at how the meaning of relationship varies among China, Japan, and Korea, who together produce three quarters of Asia-Pacific's $42 trillion dollar GDP.

1. MEANING OF RELATIONSHIP IN CHINA

The word for "relationship" in the Chinese language is *quanxi* (关系), and its importance in that society is often spoken of. Interestingly, in China, *quanxi* connections are less a relationship of familiarity and friendship and more fundamentally are bonds of mutual obligation to exchange favors and help each other.

Relationships and their built-in obligation to exchange favors are developed over time by engaging in acts for the benefit of the other party. Each party engages in those acts in order to win the recipient's favor and also to establish an indebtedness the receiving party then has an obligation to repay by returning the favors. In this manner, the two parties become locked in a relationship of mutual obligation to reciprocate assistance.

While companies in the Chinese market certainly prefer to establish and maintain *quanxi* connections with those they know well and are friends with, that familiar and personal dimension is not a requirement. A *quanxi* connection is possible with a party that one can provide assistance to and cause to become indebted to you. In these cases, the relationships are less bonds of comfort level and familiarity between parties and more utilitarian connections and expectations.

With this definition, what assurance does a company have that the other party will reciprocate? The dynamic governing this aspect of *quanxi* connections is the traditional Chinese cultural value of reciprocity (*yi* 義). Reciprocity is one of the fundamental ethical principles of China's Confucian tradition that has governed Chinese society as well as most of Asia-Pacific for centuries. It states that returning favors and acts of kindness is one of the paramount social values and obligations of all people. Failure to reciprocate favors would cause a person to lose face (one of the main social and ethical faux pas in all Confucian-based societies) and be deemed an untrustworthy and unethical person.

2. MEANING OF RELATIONSHIP IN JAPAN

In Japan, the relationship between collaborating companies means more than simply comfort level and familiarity. More fundamentally, relationship also includes trust. In fact, companies refer to their relationships with companies they collaborate with as a "trust relationship" (*shinrai kankei* 信頼関係), and it entails a *mutual commitment* to each other's corporate interests *for the long term*. It is knowing and having confidence that your business partner can be counted on to take into consideration your company's interests as well as their own as you work together—one of the hallmarks of Asia's holistic logic and outlook.

The meaning of the word trust in the Japanese language highlights and reinforces this essential meaning of relationship in Japan's *intra*-company and *inter*-company management. Accordingly, Japanese language dictionaries define the meanings to the two words comprising trust (*shin-rai*) as follows:

- *Shin* (信) To have faith in a person or thing
- *Rai* (頼) To feel that one can entrust all matters to and rely on the care of the other party

The notion that a trust relationship includes having confidence that your business partner can be counted on to take into consideration your company's interests as well as their own as you work together is deeply embedded in the significance of relationship. This is aptly expressed in the ubiquitous Japanese phrase *okagesama de* (お陰様で). Its literal meaning is "thanks to you" and is used to say "you're welcome." So, when the company yours is collaborating with expresses thanks to you for the benefits of your mutual project, you reply "thanks to you" to indicate that you could do it because both parties are equally committed to their mutual relationship and interests.

This second meaning of trust—that is, "to feel that one can entrust all matters to and rely on the care of the other party"—is another way we can see how central the idea of looking out for each other's interests is in Japanese business; it is a prerequisite to succeeding in establishing and maintaining one's collaboration with business partners. This meaning also underscores the notion that all parties are interconnected and mutually dependent, as discussed earlier.

This integral nature of trust in business relationships is markedly different from the West; in the latter, familiarity and trust are not prerequisites for commencing negotiations or business collaboration. This, of course, is not to say that trust and comfort level are not a factor when engaging in business. They certainly are. If a company lacks a comfort level or distrusts another company, they may hesitate to negotiate or initiate business collaboration, scale back their collaboration, or simply refrain from working together. Trust factor differences between Asia and the West are found in these three areas:

- The degree of importance of trust and comfort level
- How trust and comfort levels are established
- The far-reaching and long-term impact these factors have on management and business relationships

How is trust viewed in the West? In business, trust develops when a party demonstrates consistency between one's words and actions. As Harvard Business Essentials' book *Negotiating* explains:

> *Trust is created when people see tangible evidence that one's words and actions are in harmony. Therefore, avoid making commitments you may be unable to honor, and always do what you have committed to do.* —**Harvard Business Essentials. *Negotiating.* (Cambridge, MA: Harvard Business Review Press, 2003) p. 118.**

It is generally true in most countries that consistency between statements and actions creates trust. It is noteworthy that this condition is typically demonstrated *after* the joint business project commences in the West. In Asian markets, trust must be established *before* companies start a business project together. It must already exist between the two parties, or they must create it during the negotiation process.[15]

15 For a detailed analysis of the integral role of relationship in Asian negotiating, see Robert Charles Azar. *Negotiating in Asia: A Practical Guide to Succeeding in International Negotiation.* Raleigh, NC: WriteWay Publishing LLC, 2018.

Another point of distinction is that because trust is based on the parties demonstrating consistency in their transactions with each other, trust is *transactional* in the Western business. In contrast, in Asia, since trust is an integral part of the relationship that is the foundation that enables business collaboration, trust is *relational*. Trust develops based on the length, quality, and commitment of the relationship the parties establish between them. That involves many aspects beyond consistency between words and deeds.

Trust is *transactional* in Western business. In contrast, in Asia, trust is *relational*.

It is clear that the threshold level of trust requisite for companies to successfully discuss and manage business together is typically significantly greater in Asian markets than in the West. In addition, trust is significantly more involved in Asia. Let's look closely at the example of Japan.

Beyond word-deed consistency, the major features of trust relationship in Japan include the following six major facets:

1. The parties' relationship will be based on the aim of advancing the mutual interests of all companies involved.

2. Commitment to the relationship is both mutual and, as much as possible, equal.

3. Decisions regarding the business will be made with appropriate consideration of each other's circumstances and objectives.

4. Both parties' commitment to their relationship is long term.

5. Both parties' commitment to their business project is long term.

6. The mutual relationship between companies is intended to last beyond any specific business project and carry over as a ready-made foundation for business collaboration in the future.

Out of all the markets in Asia, the significance of relationship in Japan provides the greatest degree of contrast with the role of relationship in the West.

3. MEANING OF RELATIONSHIP IN KOREA

In the Korean market, relationship generally means familiarity and comfort level, the common meaning of relationship throughout most of Asia. In contrast to China or Japan, however, having a relationship is not a prerequisite for commencing a mutual business project. A quick self-introduction or introduction by a third party is sufficient for companies previously unknown to each other to begin collaborating.

In addition, relationship does not include the meaning of being mutually committed to each other's business interests or include a long-term expectation. Instead, each company focuses on pursuing its own interests while collaborating. When a joint business ceases to meet the short-term needs of a company, it is common to cease collaboration at that point. Both of these characteristics are much the same as in the West. Relationship does not act as a bond to keep the companies together. Neither the threshold of relationship needed to work together nor the significance of relationship is as high in that market.

Western firms can know that the Korean companies they are seeking to conduct business with have reached a sufficient level of familiarity and comfort with them when Korean executives refer to them as "chin-gu" (친구) when speaking in Korean. Chin-gu means "friend." Korean executives refer to those executives they have established a sufficient relationship with as "i chin-gu" (이 친구)—"this friend." In comparison, the term used in the Japanese market to refer to companies one has a trust relationship with is "partner" (パートナー). This is another indication of how the meaning of relationship as well as its degree of importance in Korean business is different and less significant in comparison to either Japan or China. Let's look further now at how the level of importance given to relationship affects managing in Asia.

B. DIFFERING IMPORTANCE OF RELATIONSHIP IN BUSINESS

We have seen how both the meaning and importance of relationship in business is quite different between the West and Asia. However, the degree of significance for relationships is not uniform in Asian markets.

The degree of priority given to relationship in Asian markets directly impacts decision-making and management of collaborative projects. For example, it is not uncommon for companies to temper their decisions and management practices out of consideration for the mutual interests of a joint business venture and its supporting relationship. Specifically, companies often select options that are better for the mutual relationship even expecting the option will yield a lower short-term return.

This dynamic is not found in the West where it is generally thought that business decisions should not be influenced by the relationship of the parties. Only decisions that are objective in that regard can be in the best interests of a firm's business.

Another factor supporting this Western management tendency is that business in the West is seen as being purpose or transaction driven; the aim of the corporation and its collaborative efforts with business partners is to achieve specific results. Accordingly, achieving the best results in business projects is the primary focus, not relationship consideration. In the final analysis, it is results that matter more than relationship.

As a consequence of these factors, Western companies generally do not give anywhere near the priority to relationship in management that Asian firms do. Western executives first experience this priority of relationship in the initial stage of interacting with Asian business companies—that is, during the negotiation process.

The seminal American book on negotiating, *Getting to Yes*, asserts giving priority importance to relationship can be counterproductive in negotiations:

> *However, any negotiation primarily concerned with the relationship runs the risk of producing a sloppy agreement.* —**Roger Fisher, William Ury and Bruce Patton, *Getting To YES: Negotiating Agreement Without Giving In* (New York: Penguin Books, 2011 third edition), p. 10.**

This Western view of relationship is aptly expressed in Harvard Business Essentials' book *Negotiation.* Interestingly, it is the section titled "Doing It Right" which suggests that including relationship at all when negotiating can be detrimental:

> *Negotiating expert Danny Ertel underscores the problems associated with negotiations in which elements of the deal and the relationship are intertwined:*
>
> > *"(Negotiators) fear that if they push too hard to get the best deal possible today, they may jeopardize their company's ability to do business with the other party in the future. Or they fear that if they pay too much attention to the relationship, they'll end up giving away too much and make a lousy deal. Though natural, such confusion is dangerous. It leaves the negotiator opened to manipulation by the other party."*
>
> *How can you avoid falling into this same trap? Ertel's advice is to distinguish between the deal and the relationship—that is, to draw a clear distinction between the components of the deal and the components of the relationship . . . ."*—**Harvard Business Essentials, *Negotiating* (Cambridge, MA: Harvard Business Review Press, 2003), pp. 115-116.**

In his Harvard Business Review book *HBR Guide to Negotiating,* Jeff Weiss commented on separating the deal from the relationship:

> *Early in the negotiation is also the right time to focus on your relationship by separating it from the essence of what's being discussed in the negotiation. We call this negotiating on two tracks . . . . People often believe they need to make concessions or forgo their interests for the sake of the relationship . . . . Conceding like this in an attempt to make the other party happy is a mistake. You're not only giving away more than you should, you're also not improving the relationship itself, so you're not even getting what you think you are "paying" for. Furthermore, you're probably making matters worse . . . .*—**Jeff Weiss, *HBR Guide to Negotiating* (Cambridge, MA: Harvard Business Review Press, 2016), p.74-75.**

According to Harvard Business Essentials' *Negotiating*, not only is including relationship considerations in negotiating problematic for a *company's* efforts to gain optimal results but it is also dangerous for the *individual negotiators* themselves who engage in the negotiations:

> *If relationships rank high among your organization's strategic goals, be forewarned that you could pay a personal price in pursuing them. Why? Because many companies still talk out of both sides of their mouths. On the one hand, they say that long-term relationships matter. On the other hand, they generally reward negotiators for delivering on monetary or other measurable values: the most advantageous settlement, the lowest-cost supplier contract, the most favorable contract terms, and so on. . . . Negotiators must separate the deal from the*

broader relationship.—**Harvard Business Essentials, *Negotiating* (Cambridge, MA: Harvard Business Review Press, 2003), p. 118-119.**

As we can see, this Western view of relationship in negotiating and business in general is antithetical to the centrality that relationship commands in indigenous Asian management practices.

In summary, relationship is very important throughout Asia including in China, Singapore, Taiwan, Thailand, Indonesia, and Vietnam. However, in most cases, not to the same degree as in Japan where the relationship and project can be equal. While relationship is important in Korea as well, it is not as strong a causal or long-term factor in management among small and medium-sized businesses as in other parts of the region.

The following figure depicts this difference in the degree of significance of relationship in business in Asia.

Figure 7: Role and Importance of Relationship in Management

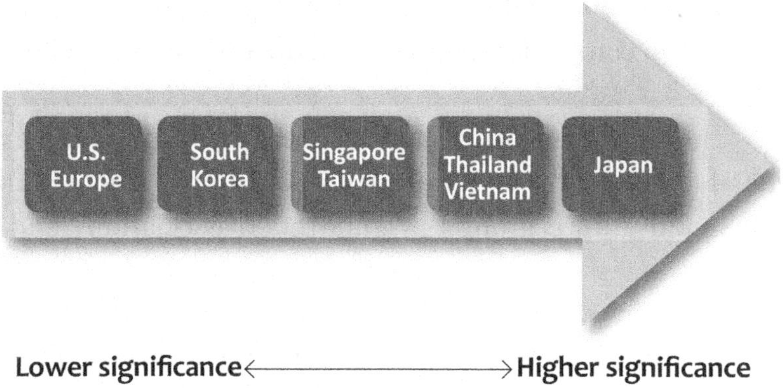

Source: Robert Charles Azar, 2021

C. INITIATING A BUSINESS RELATIONSHIP

One might wonder if a relationship is necessary for companies to work together in Asia, how companies that do not have a relationship ever have the opportunity to collaborate. In these cases, a company arranges to be introduced to the other company by a mutual third party having a preexisting relationship with both companies. As long as the third party has a sufficient mutual relationship with the two companies, it will have both the comfort level and ability to connect them through its introduction and, if required, involvement.

These third parties include:

- Companies such as banks, investment companies, business partners, consulting firms, attorneys, or similar parties.

- Government agencies and bureaucrats.

- Individuals who have a relationship with people in the two companies seeking to conduct business together.

The third category includes colleagues in the industry as well as fellow members of industry associations, school alumni, country clubs, sports groups, neighborhood associations, and the like.

While it is common in the West for alumni to utilize networks from their former colleges or graduate schools in a similar introduction manner, I was surprised to see how often the mutual connection is a former schoolmate from high school and even elementary school in Asian countries—further testament to the centrality and long-term nature of relationship in Asian societies.

After companies that do not have a pre-existing relationship are introduced, they endeavor to build their relationship both through pre-collaboration efforts to become familiar with each other and during the negotiation process. This is done concurrently with discussing the business items of interest. In these cases, developing a favorable relationship and discussing the terms of the business need to be done simultaneously as one will not proceed without the other.

D. MAINTAINING YOUR BUSINESS RELATIONSHIPS

We have established that relationship is typically necessary for companies to work together in Asia and, once started, the relationship plays a role throughout the business project—business is relationship driven. As a result, building and managing that relationship must remain an on-going priority. The following twelve actionable steps will help Western executives maximize their success in relationship management with their partners in Asia:

1. Maintain close communication with your Asian partner on a regular basis, including face-to-face meetings several times a year
2. Provide a safe harbor environment within which Asian executives feel comfortable to discuss in a thorough and timely fashion challenges that arise in the joint business and mutual relationship
3. Be proactive in identifying challenges the Asian partner confronts in promoting your business and offer your assistance for best resolving them

4. Articulate and demonstrate that your company's commitment to the Asian company and market is long term
5. Provide the partner with advance notice of developments that are related to the joint project
6. Celebrate with your Asian partner milestone achievements in the mutual business
7. Congratulate your Asian partner on their major business successes—both those that are and are not related to your joint project
8. Update your partner on new developments and breakthroughs at your company, including those unrelated to the specific joint project
9. Make opportunities for spending time together outside of official meetings by enjoying meals, after hour drinks, golf, and weekend activities
10. Express appreciation for the opportunity to work together with your Asian partner, including gifts for their senior executives
11. Send New Year's greetings at the outset of each calendar year
12. Remain polite, professional, timely, and dependable at all times, in all ways, in all matters, even with things that seem trivial from a Western perspective

II. NEGOTIATING WITH BUSINESS PARTNERS

Typically, a firm's initial substantive encounter with potential international business partners occurs when they negotiate. As is true with so many facets of management, views of the purpose and goal of negotiating vary significantly in markets around the world.

For example, in English the Latin root of negotiating is *negotiatus*, which means *"to carry on business."* As Americans, we tend to view negotiating as transactional and a means to an end—an activity to advance one's interests that will allow us to *carry on our business* with other companies. Accordingly, we engage in negotiating in a direct and deliberate manner, seeking agreements in short order.

> As is true with so many facets of management, the purpose and goal of negotiating vary significantly in markets around the world.

The country with the greatest degree of difference from the American view of negotiating in Asia is Japan, where negotiating is anything but transactional or a simple means to an end. Nor is it just an activity solely to carry on one's business.

The different meaning of negotiating in that market is clearly expressed in the word for negotiating in the Japanese language. The word *kou-shou* (交渉) means *"to associate with, to go across, to involve."* Accordingly, negotiating is different parties *associating with* the other party to get to know them, *going across* to the other party's side to get to know their interests and needs and thereby identifying mutual interests. It is also committing *to be involved* in securing those mutual interests over the long term through a trust relationship. Once this is understood, it should come as no surprise that the role of relationship in negotiating is as central as it is in Japan and that companies in that market proceed meticulously in the negotiating process compared to their Western counterparts.

The word for negotiating in China is *tán pàn* (谈判). The first character means *"to discuss"* and the second one *"to judge."* Accordingly, negotiating is seen as the means *to discuss a matter and enable a judgment* as to whether one can engage in business with the other party. In this way, negotiating is utilitarian, similar to the U.S., a means to a specific business end. Notice that relationship does not receive the same priority as utilitarian interests in China's meaning of negotiating. This is consistent with the earlier discussion of relationship commanding greater significance in the Japanese market compared to China.

In the Korean language, the word for negotiating is *hyeob-sang hada* (협상하다) and means "*to decide, settle, and fix.*" Consequently, a negotiation is expected to have a definitive outcome that *decides a matter, settles the situation, and fixes specific terms*. As you might expect from this meaning, decisions are often made on the spot during negotiating meetings, and negotiations in Korea proceed much faster than in other Asian markets, as elaborated in chapter one.

In Thailand, the word for negotiating is "*dtòr rong.*" "*Dtor*" means "*to bargain*" or "*to haggle,*" while "*rong*" means "*to carry, bear, or support.*" Negotiating is approached as *the haggling activity one bears in order to bargain* for a desired result.

The Indonesian term for negotiating is "*perundingan,*" which is *a long parley*. As negotiations are an *opportunity to consult and discuss* at length, they are expected to be long with no expectation of agreement being reached right away, as in Japan.

The Malaysian word for negotiation is "*rundingan*" and means "*talks.*" It is the *opportunity to converse and exchange information*. There is no rush to make a decision or finalize a deal.

In contrast to conversing and exchanging information, in Vietnam the word for negotiate, "*dam-phan*," means *to trade or deal*—clearly more transaction-oriented with an expectation for quicker conclusion and definitive outcome.

This pattern of the word "negotiating" carrying different meanings, goals, and nuances from country to country goes beyond America and Asia.

In Germany, the word for negotiating is "*verhandlung*" and means "*to discuss or debate*." Consequently, logical reasoning, facts, and figures weigh heavily rather than relationship considerations in negotiations in that market.

The Italian word for negotiating, "*trattativa*," means "*to talk and deal*." Accordingly, negotiations in that country are very roundabout with considerable talking, schmoozing, and dealing making.

In Spain, the term for negotiating is "*negociacion*" and means "*to bargain and transact*." As a result, negotiating there tends to be straightforward and transaction oriented.

In Brazil, "*negociacao*" means "*to deal, settle, or enroll*." Thus, negotiating entails lots of discussion and persuasion *to enroll the other party and settle upon a deal*.

As we have seen, the very meaning, purpose, and expected outcome of negotiating varies significantly country to country around the globe. To recap, the range includes:

- Simply talking
- Exchanging information
- Persuading
- Haggling and bargaining
- Making a deal
- Moving one's own business agenda forward
- Establishing a trust relationship
- Committing to both parties' mutual interests for the long term

As the very *meaning, purpose, and expected outcome* of negotiations varies so widely around the world, it is only natural that the *practice* of negotiating likewise differs country to country. This is another example of the divergent management practices around the world and the cultural values that inform them.

At one end of the spectrum, the goal of a negotiation is to gain as many of your firm's business interests as possible, while ceding as few as possible. Negotiations—and business in general—are approached as a zero-sum game whereby it is commonplace for one company's objectives to be obtained at the other party's expense. This style of negotiating is prevalent in the U.S. and other markets where it is viewed as a means to an end.

At the other end of the spectrum, we find the collectivist

approach where negotiating and business are viewed in a holistic manner as a process of give and take in which both companies recognize and try to accommodate each other's business interests while endeavoring to secure the long-term success of the joint project.

Why is the approach to business partner relationships so different between Asia and the West? One of the most fundamental reasons for this major dissimilarity in management practices is what drives business in these two regions.

In the U.S. and Europe, for example, we have noted that business is *transaction driven*. That is, two or more companies agree to collaborate to achieve the specific business objectives of a mutual project. Typically, those goals are clearly delineated in the business agreement the companies sign at the outset of a project. These agreements spell out the specific roles and responsibilities of each party in considerable detail, and by signing the agreement the companies commit themselves to performing those specified tasks. They are not responsible for or obligated to provide any work or services beyond what the agreement specifically calls them to do.

In contrast, we noted in Asian markets business is *relationship driven*. Business is conducted based on the foundation of the relationship between the companies involved. Accordingly, due consideration needs to be given to relationships at every stage of business collaboration. As one executive in Thailand put it: "Invest in the relationship and bottom-line profit will naturally follow." International executives must keep these different drivers in mind right from initial negotiations between their corporation and their potential Asian partners. Let's take a quick look at this.[16]

As a consequence of the preference to conduct business based on a favorable relationship, negotiating in Asia takes place on two distinct levels:

- Working out the business specifics of the joint project
- Creating a sense of partnership and mutual benefit between the two firms by building a relationship for long-term collaboration

Asian negotiators pursue these two objectives simultaneously and in parallel. Think of these two parts of negotiating as the two rails of a railroad track. A train can only move forward if both rails are laid in parallel and at the same time. Likewise, negotiations with Asian firms will only move forward when progress with both the terms of the business and the relationship of the parties occur in tandem.

This dual pursuit is the reason they engage in so much relationship building activity during the course of the negotiation, such as discussion of topics unrelated to the specifics of the proposed business, long dinners, evening drinks, and golf or other weekend activities. It is also one of the reasons Western executives feel little progress is made after hours of discussion, as in the example of the Alamance Corporation in chapter one. The consequence of satisfying this dual purpose is another reason why the pace of negotiations is significantly slower in most Asian markets than in the West.

16 For a detailed analysis of the differences and challenges in negotiating in Asia and how to successfully navigate them, see Robert Charles Azar. *Negotiating in Asia: A Practical Guide to Succeeding in International Negotiation*. Raleigh, NC: WriteWay Publishing LLC., 2018.

Western executives are well acquainted with this first part of negotiating—working out the specifics of the joint business project—but they give far less attention to relationship building. Why is this the case? In the West, once the purpose of the joint business project is completed, the parties wish each other well and go their separate ways. The situation can be quite different in Asia. As we have pointed out, the mutual relationship commonly outlasts an individual business project. Through negotiating project specifics and building a business relationship, both companies lay the foundation to work together to enhance their mutual interests and well-being long term. This means both through the initial business project as well as subsequent ones. This is a fundamental difference between businesses that are transaction driven and businesses that are relationship driven.

In Asian markets, the relationship-driven approach to business is significantly more inclusive, mutual-benefit oriented, and broader-based in focus than in the transaction-driven business of the West. It is, therefore, not unusual for collaborating corporations to discuss their broader goals and needs beyond those of the immediate business project. As a consequence, Asian management, including managing customers and business partners, is more holistic and comprehensive in nature and greatly differs from the more singular focus on one's own bottom-line interests in America and Europe.

In negotiating, for instance, Western negotiators give priority concern to the needs of their own company and advocate for them. They generally list their items of interest and determine the most logical and beneficial order in which to pursue them in the negotiation. With their corporate interests listed in the most rational and advantageous manner possible, Western negotiators pursue them in linear fashion, moving from one item to the next on the list. Agreement to one item helps move the negotiation forward, presumably offering a better position from which to support and win agreement to upcoming points. As these subsequent points are often based on the preceding items, an inability to come to agreement on a topic can result in the negotiations slowing down or becoming derailed.

Utilizing a holistic approach, Asian negotiators, in contrast, commonly move from one topic to another in the negotiation, often without the logical order that Western executives are accustomed to following. When focusing on the joint project and the broader interests of the mutual relationship rather than the immediate negotiating topics, discussions generally cover items not included in the more narrowly focused interest list of Western firms. As a result, more topics are covered within the comprehensive approach of Asian negotiating and that causes negotiations to proceed more slowly and last longer. The differing methodological approaches to the same negotiation often cause frustration for both parties due to the different topics, the number and incongruity of the order of topics discussed, and divergent outcome goals.

Based on the priority given to relationship, mutual interest, and comprehensive considerations, the holistic approach in Asian business applies not only to negotiating but to most other facets of management as well. Operating with a narrower focus on the best interests of their own firm, Western executives utilize this rational, linear approach likewise not just in negotiating but in other areas of management as well; it calls for decisions to be made based on what is in the best interests of the company's bottom line seen from an objective perspective commonly referred to as "rational decision-making."

With this focus, Western decision-making in management strives to select the best of the available options for each item, one at a time and in sequential order. Options are either better or worse. Favorable or unfavorable. Desirable or undesirable. Yes or no. Decisions are often approached in that clear, rational, binary fashion.

Meanwhile, the holistic approach that drives Asian management likewise underpins not only negotiating but also decision-making, as discussed earlier. As opposed to considering individual items one at a time, Asian executives view and decide based on selecting the best option for the entire project at large, including all departments involved and the entire corporation in a holistic framework. When applicable and feasible, that includes taking into account the interests of all involved stakeholders.

These two greatly differing approaches are ever-present in East-West management. At a minimum, they are a source of continual misunderstanding and frustration. In the worst-case scenario, these differences often cause collaboration with Asian business partners to fall apart and the morale and productivity of in-house Asian employees to decline.

Western executives need to be cognizant of these fundamentally different dynamics governing the managing of business partners and customers in Asian markets. The problem is that international managers typically are not aware of these differences and that their bottom-line performance is negatively impacted by them. How, then, can companies deal with these management differences? One highly recommended solution is to have in-house experts who are aware of and can effectively navigate divergent management practices. This strategy is analyzed in chapter nine.

III. COMPROMISE, CONCESSIONS, AND BARGAINING

A. THE SIGNIFICANCE OF COMPROMISE, CONCESSIONS, AND BARGAINING

With an approach to management that focuses on the long term, gives significant priority to win-win relationships, utilizes a holistic viewpoint, and values companies doing what changing business conditions require more than being bound to the detailed terms of agreements, it is expected that both parties will be favorably inclined to make compromises and concessions as they negotiate and later jointly manage business operations. But just how much compromise and how many concessions are required?

The degree required in Asia varies from market to market. In the Japanese market, for example, compromise is viewed as being an essential part of a "trust relationship" as a trust relationship has at its core the commitment to the mutual interest of both companies as well as their joint business. Not compromising is contrary to this fundamental expectation. A company that will not compromise lacks "sincerity" in the Asian context and is not committed to trying to accommodate the interests of the other party and their mutual business. Such a company demotes itself as a viable partner. As we can see, trust being precluded in Japan due to unwillingness to compromise is quite different from trust being prevented in America due to inconsistency between word and action.

In addition, as each company is expected to be guided by the mutual interests of both companies and their joint project, padding one's positions and haggling are generally not viewed positively in Japan.

Compromise and concessions are also expected in China. However, in contrast to Japan, haggling is commonly engaged in. As a result, companies in China typically pad their positions in discussions and negotiations, sometimes to a degree even greater than Western firms do.

In Western companies, concessions and bargaining are often agreed to at the same time and seen as one-for-one swaps—I agree to that term you are proposing and in exchange you agree to the item I am seeking. In China, compromises, concessions, and bargaining are often not direct one-for-one exchanges. Rather they are a negotiating tool whereby several lower priority items are bundled and given away together later in the discussion in order to gain high priority items.

This usually happens at the final stage of the negotiation. It is common for discussions to drag on for an extended period with little apparent progress and then in the last phase, Chinese companies will suddenly agree to compromises and concessions to several items at once. In contrast, concessions and bargaining are utilized as needed throughout management discussions in the West. This is another reason why in Asian markets negotiations and management decisions take longer and very lengthy discussions seem to leave substantive matters undecided.

It is important for Western executives to keep this dynamic in mind; otherwise, it is common to become discouraged when protracted discussions seem to have accomplished little. When the discussion reaches the critical mass stage for

Chinese executives—that is, when they arrive at the point where they are ready to give a decision on several topics at once—the negotiation gets catapulted into the next stage, demonstrating that Western and Asian executives engage in compromises and concessions at different stages in the negotiations as well as for different reasons. This is another area in which Westerners and Asians utilize different types of approaches, rationales, and logic in management.

Western and Asian executives engage in compromises and concessions at different stages in the negotiations as well as for different reasons.

As in China, companies in Singapore and Korea typically engage in posturing to a much greater degree than Japanese firms, including padding one's negotiating positions. In addition, Korean negotiators are quite passionate and persistent hagglers. In contrast to the relatively staid negotiating common in China, Japan, Singapore, Taiwan, and Vietnam, Korean negotiators often engage in haggling and bargaining with a boisterousness and forcefulness that belies the traditional name the Korean people affectionately use referring to their homeland—"The Land of the Morning Calm" (*cho-sun* 조선). While boisterousness is not viewed favorably in Singapore, bargaining and haggling are, and they are commonplace. However, a negotiator raising his voice, appearing to be upset, or engaging in an emotional outburst is viewed negatively in most Asian markets other than small and medium-sized firms in Korea.

Figure 8: Use of Haggling and Bargaining in Negotiating

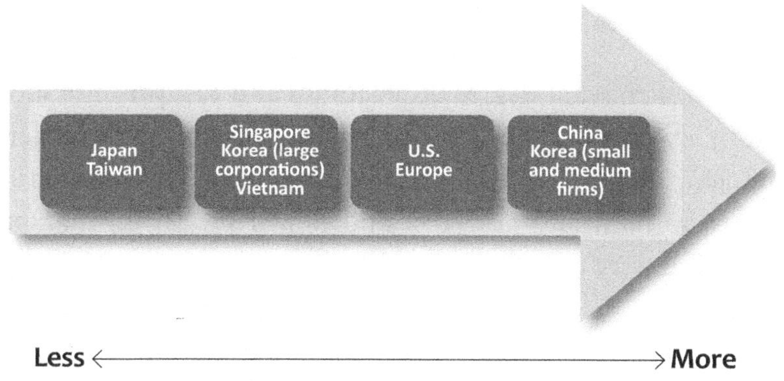

Source: Robert Charles Azar, 2021

Compromising is generally not seen as weakness in Asia but rather as strength—and shows that you are a strong business partner. Why? Compromising is a clear indication that you are committed to the long-term success of your joint business project. It also demonstrates that your relationship with the other company is a priority for you. You are "putting your money where your mouth is." Accordingly, compromise is an important way in which Western executives can demonstrate to Asian executives that not only the joint business project is important to your company but so also is your relationship with them. With this in mind, it is highly advisable to start negotiations with several "give away" items that you have prepared in advance that are likely to be of interest to the other party.

The Asian negotiating dynamic of compromising, together with its commitment to the mutual relationship and the long-term success of the project, often causes foreign executives to feel bewildered. Just how much do you need to compromise? It is not necessary to compromise on or agree to every proposal put forth. Give and take is expected from both sides, and both parties must be comfortable with compromises made if the agreement is to be viable and have longevity.

So then what degree of flexibility and compromise should Western executives demonstrate when negotiating in order to show "sincerity" (or genuineness of purpose in Western culture)? There is no hard and fast rule, and it will vary from market to market, industry to industry, and company to company. As a general guideline, I have found that the degree of flexibility that is expected rises with importance of the matter. In the end, striking a sensible balance between the needs of the project and the realities of your company is always a reasonable—and the only sustainable—approach. This can only be decided on a case-by-case basis. It is recommended to proceed slowly when you are facing such an uncertainty. My clients often find it can be beneficial to forego their customary linear decision-making and adopt the Asian approach and hold off on major compromises until the late stages of the discussion.

B. AVOIDING COMPROMISE

> "Not being contractually obligated" does not translate well culturally and, more importantly, relationally in Asia.

Given the importance in Asia of compromise, how can Western companies avoid agreeing to a request for a compromise? The "we are not contractually obligated to do that" response that is commonplace in the West, for example, can be counterproductive in Asia as it makes your company come across as inflexible and, rather than thinking about the needs of the mutual project, focused only on your company. Simply put, the notion of "not being contractually obligated" does not translate well culturally and, more importantly, relationally in Asia.

During the course of managing joint business projects, it is not uncommon for items to arise where compromise is not possible for your company. In that case, endeavor to provide your reasoning in a way that translates well culturally and relationally. This is an area where, as discussed in chapter nine, a cultural facilitator plays a crucial role in managing business in Asia. When unable to compromise on a given point, it can be helpful to offer a concession on another item instead, even an unrelated item.

I have found that the following tactics work well to avoid agreeing to unwanted requests or proposals:

- If applicable, take the position that a proposal goes against the established corporate policies of your company. Asians respect this position and realize nothing can be done about it. This reason translates well culturally and usually lays that proposal to rest.

- Reply by saying that your company thought about that option but never came to a decision about it. Offer that the matter can be discussed further in your company. This is an effective way of deflecting the issue while demonstrating flexibility with your business partner.

- Respond by saying that your company has never considered that before but will look into it. When all else fails, this catchall reply is generally favorably received. As discussed in chapter two, decision-making in Asian companies generally includes all the departments affected by a proposal and, consequently, takes a considerable amount of time. If you reply to Asian counterparts with this response, you loudly signal that a lengthy time period will be required for your company to examine the proposal and be in a position to respond to it.

- Once the project has begun, reply to additional proposals and requests by taking the position that in the West the terms of an agreement are not changed once the project begins. However, given the importance you place on your mutual relationship, you will discuss with your fellow executives if it is possible to explore this matter *as a special case*. This allows an executive to signal that acquiescence may not be likely but that your company values and respects its relationship with your Asian counterpart.

C. DEGREES OF COMPROMISE NECESSARY

How does the degree of compromise in Asian management compare with the West? In America, for instance, the goal of winning one's desired terms is given greater importance than relationship in negotiating. It is for that reason that the authors admonish against compromise for the sake of the mutual relationship in the book *Getting to Yes: Negotiating Agreement Without Giving In* when they write: "Our point is that you should not give in for the purpose of trying to improve a relationship" (p. 161). The book's subtitle highlights that management approach as well—*Negotiating Agreement Without Giving In*.

In its *HBR Guide to Negotiating*, Harvard Business Review comments on this American negotiating practice by advising that negotiators should avoid "*. . . sacrificing your interests in order to preserve the relationship. Deal with the relationship separately.*" [17]

This advice is given in the book's section titled "Watch Out for Common Mistakes," again indicating how low a priority is given to relationship. While this dynamic is applicable in Western nations, international executives need to be aware that this is often not the case in Asian markets.

Likewise, Harvard's *Negotiation* sums up the common Western view of compromise in the context of promoting relationship as follows:

> *The best advice about concessions is to avoid the impulse to make them. . . . Remember, too, that deal making isn't about making friends.* —**Harvard Business Essentials, *Negotiating* (Cambridge, MA: Harvard Business Review Press, 2003), p. 54.**

It is critically important to realize that while relationship may imply friendship and a history of working together in the West, the meaning is totally different in Asia as we have seen over and over in this book. What is meant by relationship is so much broader, more fundamental, and consequential in traditional Asian management.

At the same time, we have seen noteworthy degrees of how relationship's import and impact on business varies throughout

17 Jeff Weiss, *HBR Guide to Negotiating* (Cambridge, MA: Harvard Business Review Press, 2016), p. 101.

the region as the following figure illustrates.

Figure 9: The Relationship Spectrum: Varying Degrees of Importance and Impact of Relationship in Business

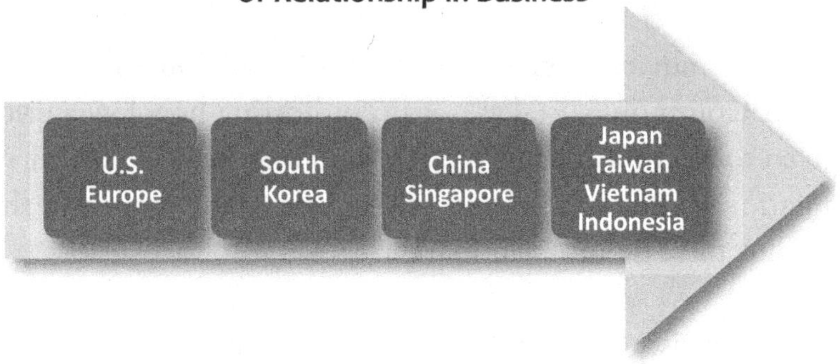

MEANING OF RELATIONSHIP

Past experience working together → Comfort level → Commitment to project → Commitment to relationship → Long-term duration

Source: Robert Charles Azar, 2021

I have witnessed numerous instances where Asian executives ceased both negotiations and on-going business projects, walking away from multi-million-dollar deals, because they were not able to develop the requisite relationship with foreign companies. As I developed relationships with these executives over time and was able to discuss this with them, the reason they would give is that the business is not worth it. They explained that since their interest is in long-term success, knowing that both parties are committed to the relationship as well as the project for the long term is essential. Their concern was that without such a dual commitment, how could they discuss and resolve the multiplicity of issues that inevitably arise over time in a business venture in ways that are best for the two companies and their mutual business?

Another factor at play is that Asian markets are significantly less litigious than Western countries. When a business reaches an impasse or breaks down, companies in the U.S. and Europe typically remedy the situation through the court system. This is not the case in Asia where the parties are expected to discuss and work out the issue between them in good faith, a cultural norm deeply embedded in Asian societies due to the centuries-old emphasis on one's obligation to uphold social harmony, to avoid conflict, and to avoid causing anyone to lose face.

Even in Asian nations with well-established rule of law societies, litigation is commonly looked down upon by society. Instead, customary social values of harmony require companies to resolve their differences between them. This is why Asian nations have considerably fewer lawyers than Western nations. Japan, for example, is the Asian nation with the longest experience and most fully developed western style legal system, as it adopted Western law in 1868. Despite the country's population equaling forty percent of the U.S. population today, Japan has only five percent of the number of attorneys as the U.S.

Given the customary need to work out differences of opinion between business partners in good faith, it is essential that companies forge a relationship sufficient to make that possible, one that accounts for the interests of both parties and is long term. All these factors contribute to relationship being a critical deal maker or deal breaker in numerous facets of Asian business. This dynamic in Asian markets further illustrates how the importance of relationships can result in a greater degree of compromises and concessions.

Chapter 4

UNDERSTANDING PARTNER AND CUSTOMER EXPECTATIONS

I. DIFFERENT FUNCTION OF DISCUSSION AND MEANING OF AGREEMENT

Asian management's holistic logic also results in the region's different approach to discussions, the nature of discussions, and the resulting agreements. In the U.S. and Europe, for instance, we approach discussions by organizing and discussing topics in the following manner:

- Consecutively in an order that makes sense from what we consider to be a logical viewpoint

- In a way that will enable the discussion to proceed in a timely and time-efficient manner

- Such that decisions can be made quickly—even right on the spot—and in a matter-of-fact manner that moves business forward expeditiously

- With a preference for direct, less nuanced discussions and decisions

- Such that decisions often result in winners and losers

In contrast, discussion topics are pursued with the following holistic characteristics in Asian markets:

- In what appears to international executives to be in haphazard or in disjointed order

- At a much slower-pace that Western companies often interpret as less productive and an inefficient use of time

- In a manner designed to foster stronger mutual relationship in addition to specific business items

- With a preference for indirect, more nuanced discussions and decisions

- In a manner to be inclusive and for the mutual benefit of the parties

In the West, we typically address specific terms from the

outset of the discussion. Agreement on the initial items sets the stage for and enables agreement on subsequent details; agreement on each point drives the discussion forward creating a sense of momentum and that progress is being made. Progress can be measured in a quantifiable manner by checking off and counting how many topics have been covered out of the total.

In Asia, general topics, rather than specific terms, are often emphasized in the early stage of discussion. Specific terms receive greater attention later commensurate with progress in relationship building between the parties. Why? As a favorable relationship is the foundation of and prerequisite for business collaboration, a lack of progress in relationship building negates the need to discuss and agree on details. This approach makes it difficult to measure progress in a quantifiable way by counting specific topics covered and agreed to. This fundamental difference in how discussions are approached and engaged in typically leaves international executives thinking that meetings and discussions had less value than they actually did.

Another consequence of Asia's holistic logic is that the meaning of agreement reached through discussion is different. Asian executives discuss topics to *clarify and prioritize the facts* of the matter for decision-making, to *promote mutual understanding of each* item and its implications within the greater context of how all related parties will be impacted, and to *reach an understanding among the parties involved* as to what is in the best interest of the entire situation. This allows the parties the ability to respond to the changing needs of the project over time and supports and drives Asia's holistic management. As a consequence, details are often not covered to the same degree or decided upon early on in discussions compared to the West.

In addition, this fundamental difference has profound impact on not only what the aim of discussion is but what a decision means. This is often a stumbling block for international firms. In the West, when parties agree to an item, they accept it and incorporate it into their action plans for execution. In contrast, Asian companies utilizing holistic management aim to reach an agreement on an item's importance, but that does not necessarily mean that they fully agree with all the particulars related to executing it. It is the difference between agreeing on the level of importance of a matter versus agreeing on how to implement it.

Consequently, "agreement" in Asia does not always equate with "acceptance" and "enactment" as it is typically viewed in the West. This is one of the fundamental reasons why Asian executives readily seek to return to and want to change items previously discussed and "agreed upon" even long after business contracts were duly executed. The reason is that the importance of those points was accepted without necessarily fully committing to the specifics of their implementation.

"Agreement" in Asia does not always equate with "acceptance" and "enactment" as it is typically viewed in the West.

Western executives should prepare themselves so they are not surprised by this facet of Asia's holistic management. From the perspective of their Asian counterparts, the Western executives should be willing to modify previously agreed to terms because doing so is in the long-term interests of the mutual business project and the relationship that supports it.

II. DISSIMILAR DYNAMICS IN MANAGING BUSINESS PARTNER RELATIONSHIPS

A. CONTRACTUAL VS. RELATIONAL OBLIGATION

Another result of Asia's holistic management is that firms in the region do not specify the responsibilities of each party in the detail that Western firms do in business agreements. While roles and general areas of responsibility are discussed and agreed upon, they often are not delineated with the degree of detail and specificity that Western executives are accustomed to having in contracts. From a Western perspective, this is counterintuitive because even though negotiations involve significantly longer amounts of time, the resulting agreement has substantially less content and fewer pages when written by their Asian partners. There are two reasons for this.

- First, realizing that the challenges any business project faces will, quite naturally, change over time as conditions evolve, the Asian approach is to focus on the needs of and mutual commitment to the total project instead of on specific tasks. It is expected that companies will do, within reason and as their resources allow, what is required by the project as business conditions alter over time.

- Second, as a result of business being based on a collaborative relationship, it is also expected that the parties will act in good faith and make additional investments to engage in tasks that become required over time.

Because Western negotiations focus on specific roles and tasks of the companies involved, U.S. and European business agreements excel in making sure that the participants engage in the specific roles and tasks delineated in it. In contrast, the Asian approach excels in making sure each participant is committed to the project and to performing its requisite roles and tasks over time—another way in which long-term perspective impacts business practices in the region. The Asian approach affords the companies involved greater flexibility to meet the needs of the project as those needs evolve in the future. The Western approach less so.

On the other hand, because the Western approach locks each company into specified roles and tasks they are contractually obligated to provide as delineated in the business agreement, it gives the company a way to avoid any additional tasks not included in the agreement. This can be a valuable safeguard in the event of requests the company is not interested in or the project is not going well and the company wishes to exit the venture.

In contrast, since Asian companies are committed to carrying out project tasks that can be reasonably expected of them over time because they are committed to the long-term success of the joint venture as well as to the mutual relationship, Asian firms are on the hook for a lot more than Western businesses are.

In summary, while the Western approach to negotiating and working with business partners puts companies in a position to be *contractually* obligated, Asian management practices make companies *relationally* obligated. This difference has far-reaching consequences for how business is managed in the two regions as discussed throughout this book.

Being relationally obligated to a joint business project for the long term is another reason for the Asian preference for negotiating more slowly than their Western counterparts and for wanting to establish a sufficient comfort level and strong relationship before they decide to engage in business with a new business partner.

From the Asian perspective, the importance of building that favorable working relationship has additional practical value. It is very easy to start subsequent projects together once a relationship is in place. When a company needs to secure a partner for a new project, it is much more likely to prefer a company with whom it already has laid the foundation for a relationship than with a company it has not.

As a result of these factors, discussions and negotiating in Asia require more time than in other regions. These factors also contribute to why Asian companies are slow to sign a business agreement, given the greater degree of obligation they are taking on. It is advisable that Western executives keep these fundamental differences in mind and appropriately prepare for them as they manage business partners in Asia.

By way of recent example, when the trade negotiations between the U.S. and China amid their tariff war derailed in May 2019, U.S. negotiators cited two major reasons for this as reported in the Wall Street Journal:

- First, Chinese negotiators wanted to sign what the U.S. government described as a summary of the discussions, not a detailed document containing all the points the two parties had "agreed" to. From the context of U.S. business culture, this is seen as China not being serious about the deal and raises questions regarding China's trustworthiness.

From the Chinese perspective, it is not necessary to have an agreement with the level of detail and specifics that Western entities are accustomed to. For them, since business is based on relationship, it is understood that China will honor what has been agreed to and be flexible to meet changing conditions in the future. As China's negotiators put it, this was "a matter of honor: The U.S. should trust Beijing to make the changes they said they would make. . . ."

- Second, U.S. government officials claimed that China reneged on their agreement to individual points made earlier in the negotiation. "Throughout the negotiations, there have been tensions. U.S. officials complained in February that China was reneging on previously agreed items, the same dynamic that resurfaced in recent days." From China's perspective, however, it was not reneging but acting in a manner consistent with the region's holistic logic and the different meaning of agreement prevalent in Asian management, as discussed above.[18]

China's positions are understandable and quite natural from the perspective of Asia's holistic logic. As it is often possible to make final decisions on specific items only when the whole

18 Lingling Wei, Vivian Salama, Michael C. Bender and Bob Davis. *Wall Street Journal*. "Frustration, Miscalculation: Inside the U.S.-China Trade Impasse." May 13, 2019. Page A1.

picture of what is being considered has been discussed in full—which is in the final stage of the discussions—it is common for Asian negotiators to alter positions they "agreed to" earlier.

B. BUSINESS AGREEMENTS: FIXED VS. FLUID

In the U.S. and Europe, once the terms of a business project are finalized in a signed agreement, the terms are basically set in stone. It is understood and expected that the major terms will not be renegotiated once they have been agreed upon, barring an emergency. As discussed, Western executives and governments quickly find that this is not the case in Asia where signed agreements are viewed as being fluid and not fixed.

In the U.S. and Europe, agreements are the framework within and the foundation upon which business is conducted. In short, an agreement provides the complete and final understanding of the business project and how each party is to perform. The notion that the agreement totally governs the project and is the final understanding of the participating parties is clearly seen in the fact that one of the last sections of most business agreements in the West states that the agreement represents the full and complete understanding of the parties and supersedes any and all previous discussions, agreements, and understandings, written or oral. In other words, the final agreement is "the be-all and end-all."

Throughout Asia, an agreement is often more akin to what is referred to as a memorandum of understanding in the West, namely a statement of mutual intent to work together. While a memorandum of understanding covers the area of proposed mutual collaboration, they generally do not include implementation specifics to a great degree. Accordingly, the terms of the agreement are not written in stone but are a statement of the parties' general understanding and aspiration. As Wu Min, an executive at a Fortune 500 Chinese corporation, expressed it to me:

> *How can anyone know what the future brings? The only thing we know about the future is that it will be different from today. Does it make sense, then, to say that in the future we must be bound by terms agreed to today, when those terms may no longer apply to our business?*

Again, we see how "rational decision-making" by management in Asia and the West can be inherently different and employ dissimilar logic and approaches. And these two types of rational decision-making are in constant contention, causing friction, disagreement, loss of commitment, and ultimately the breakdown of business between companies in the two regions.

> "Rational decision-making" by management in Asia and the West can be inherently different and employ dissimilar logic and approaches.

It is necessary for international executives to address these differences at the very outset of discussions or managing a project with Asian partners and come to agreement on which approach will govern your collaboration. While setting ground rules at the outset may not preclude Asian companies from reverting to traditional methods, clarifying and agreeing on them places your company in a significantly stronger position from which to resist and decline than would otherwise be the case.

Far from monolithic, the degree of prevalence of the view that agreements are changeable varies throughout the region as the following figure illustrates.

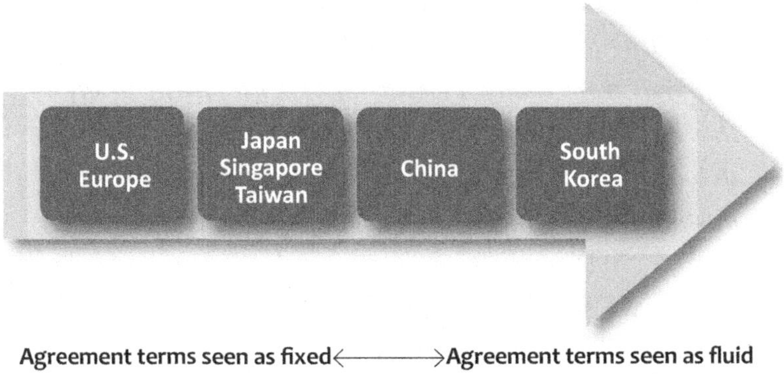

Figure 10: Terms of Agreements: Fixed vs. Fluid

Source: Robert Charles Azar, 2021

C. FLUID MEETING APPOINTMENTS

When I first began to engage in business in the Korean market, I was surprised to learn that not only are business agreements considered fluid but that business appointments likewise are not always firm commitments that have been "agreed upon." Time after time I would make appointments to meet with company owners or executives only to experience them not showing up. Not only did they not honor the appointments, they did not even contact my office to say they would not be able to keep the appointment or to reschedule it.

Sensing my frustration with this situation, one day Mr. Nam, the native Korean vice president of my company's operations in Korea, explained that appointments are not fixed meetings but are simply expressions of an interest to work together. They are just like business agreements in this regard. While true more of small and medium-sized companies than large professional corporations, it is an interesting characteristic of the Korean market that highlights the different meaning of what has been agreed to.

How can international executives navigate this difference? I have found the following three measures to work well dealing with fluid meeting appointments.

First, it is worth the effort to send a fax or a letter by messenger—not a text or email—one or two days in advance confirming a meeting. I do not recommend using a text message or an email as it will be hidden in the Inbox of the executive and only be seen by him. He may or may not bother to reply or even read it. Sending a letter or fax will result in the executive's staff seeing it. Now it becomes an official company communication that is less likely to be ignored.

The staff will make sure the appointment is on the executive's calendar. In addition, when they discuss the letter or fax with the executive, the meeting takes on new importance. It graduates from merely being a one-to-one item to being an official company activity involving other members of the firm.

Second, have a Korean member of your team call the executive to confirm the meeting the day before. Being able to read the nuances of their own native business culture, that person will be able to more accurately ascertain whether the meeting is simply an expression of interest or a firm appointment. In the event you do not have a native speaker on your team, the duty manager or concierge professional at the hotel where you are staying will be happy to assist you. I have utilized this option numerous times throughout Asia and never experienced any reluctance on their part to help. Since you are a guest at their hotel, they see assisting with this as part of their holistic customer service.

Third, set the venue for meeting at the Korean executives' location. This is especially true of all initial meetings with their company. Doing so precludes the executives from "not showing up"—you are at *their* office. They will certainly meet with you at that time, if they are in. If Mr. Park, for instance, is out of the office and you show up rightfully saying that you have an appointment with him and show the confirmation letter or fax you sent the previous day, the entire staff is embarrassed to the point they will immediately track down Mr. Park and have him return to the company to meet with you. It is one way Western executives can skillfully play "the foreigner card."

It should be noted that while meeting appointments can be fluid with small and medium-sized companies in the Korean market, this is not a factor with large professional corporations.

III. CUSTOMER SERVICE

Companies engage with and manage their customers in two primary ways: through the products they produce and the customer service they provide. Customer service, product quality, and end-user preferences vary significantly across international markets. Among Asian markets, the most stringent standards and customer relationship management (CRM) practices can be found in the Japanese market. Let's take a closer look.

The difference in customer service standards between Japan and the U.S., for example, is aptly illustrated in the following sayings: The customer is king (U.S.) and the customer is god (Japan).

These two sayings epitomize the different levels of importance of and commitment to customers in the two countries. The Japanese saying demonstrates the heightened priority management places on satisfying the customer. Matsushita Konosuke, the founder and CEO of the Panasonic Corporation, expressed this clearly in a quote shared in a biography about his professional legacy:

> *"The goods we make here every day . . . are like children we raise with tender care. Selling them is like seeing those children grow up and go out into the world. It is only natural, then, that we should be concerned about how they're getting on in their lives, and to go and see for ourselves."*
>
> *He believed that maintaining this concern for what you produce is the first step to building an extra ordinary supplier–client relationship into a stronger link based on mutual trust.* —**PHP Institute, Inc., *Matsushita Konosuke (1894-1989): His Life & Legacy* (Tokyo: PHP Institute, Inc., 1994), page 52.**

Notice the importance Matsushita gives to mutual trust, the significance of which was discussed earlier. Superior customer service is integral to establishing and maintaining the trust relationship with the end-user.

Matsushita took the position that customer service should be viewed as even more important than a company's product itself. In another quote, Matsushita explained:

> *After-sales service is the key to keeping your customers. No matter how good the product you put on the market, if you do not provide equally good after-sales service, the customer will not come back. He will shower you with complaints and then go elsewhere. In many respects service is more important than the product itself.* **—PHP Institute, Inc., *Matsushita Konosuke (1894-1989): His Life & Legacy* (Tokyo: PHP Institute, Inc., 1994), page 70.**

The customer-centric focus of management in many Asian markets is aptly expressed in the following sales slogan of the Toyota Motor Corporation, "The user comes first, the dealer second, and the manufacturer third."[19]

Japanese have a saying that aptly expresses the essence of customer service in their country: *omotenashi* (おもてなし). The literal dictionary meaning is "hospitality." However, the management practice that grew out of this cultural norm means to have the mindset to look at all things from the perspective of the end user; to prepare all things from the perspective of the client—from manufacturing to presentation to customer service. It further means to anticipate and take care of every potential need of your customer before he or she articulates them.

19 Satoshi Hino. *Inside The Mind of Toyota: Management Principles for Enduring Growth*. New York: Productivity Press, 2006, page 12.

IV. QUALITY STANDARDS

Once again, the Japanese market provides the greatest contrast to product quality standards in the U.S. and Europe. In the West, product defect rates vary greatly from country to country and industry to industry. In the U.S., for example, defect rate percentages can reach as high as double digit levels and this is accepted by both manufacturers and consumers.

In contrast, companies in Japan have no tolerance for defective products going to market. This "zero tolerance" policy has become closely studied and emulated all over the world since the 1980s. As a result, the Japanese market—manufacturer and consumer—does not accept products with defects or imperfections. As Inamori Kazuo, the founder of the Kyocera Corporation and one of Japan's foremost business leaders today, explained:

> *Demands for superior product quality today are such that defective goods are altogether unacceptable. In Sales, Production, Research and Development, and all other processes, perfection is demanded.* —**Inamori Kazuo, *Amoeba Management* (Boca Raton, Florida: CRC Press, 2013), page 74.**

While respected by manufacturers all over the world, this zero-tolerance policy can present a daunting level of quality that international firms have to meet if they want to succeed in Japan. Failure to meet that product quality standard has done in many foreign companies' efforts to engage in business in the world's third largest economy.

Meeting this quality standard can require varying

investment levels of time, resources, capital, and manpower. When foreign products are already at or close to those standards, only minor product adjustments may be needed. In those cases, typically little or no additional product investment is needed to sell those products in Japan. In cases where the product quality needs major improvement, the investment can be significant. So significant, in fact, that meeting those quality standards can render that product unprofitable and, therefore, not worth pursuing in the Japanese market. The costs in time and resources to meet expected product quality requirements have kept many international products out of this Asian market.

Meeting Japan's product quality standards requires international company management to examine numerous aspects of their overall business operations. For example, the company needs to examine not only how much it would need to invest to improve its ingredient or component quality but also look at its manufacturing processes, packaging, product handling, shipping methods, storage options, and other factors that determine the quality of the products that ultimately end up in the hands of the consumer.

In the experience of many Western companies, making the adjustments needed to meet the more stringent quality levels of the Japanese market turns out to bring windfall benefit to their global business operations. Typically, the improvements that Western management makes to engage in business in Japan are subsequently applied to the company's operations worldwide. The result is often improved manufacturing processes, products with a higher level of quality, and greater sales and customer satisfaction worldwide, all of which enhance the company's global competitive standing.

It is often said that Japan can be a gateway to the rest of Asia and the reason assumed for this is its geographic location. However, Japan's regional neighbors view it as a gateway to Pacific markets because of its more stringent quality standards. If the product of a Western company succeeds in Japan, then it usually has already passed the regulatory and quality requirements of other Asian markets.

PART 2

SUCCESSFULLY MANAGING YOUR BUSINESS IN ASIA

Strategies and Protocols for Maximizing Success

Chapter 5

BEST PRACTICE STRATEGIES FOR SUCCESS

"Getting rich is glorious."—**Deng Xiaoping, leader of China from 1978-1992 responsible for putting in place the country's market economy reforms**

Ever since Premiere Deng Xiaoping reversed the economic policies of the initial leaders of the People's Republic of China in 1980, seeking wealth has been officially sanctioned. Western companies did not lose time in seeking to likewise benefit from China's move from a closed central state planned and controlled economy to a mixed open market economy. This chapter examines the critically important topic of what products and business partners are most advantageous when engaging in business in Asia; which employees are most desirable for working in foreign markets; the internal company impediments to succeeding in international management; and the six market determinants of the types of management found in international markets.

I. PACKING YOUR MOST IMPORTANT PIECE OF LUGGAGE

One of the most fundamental mistakes I have witnessed U.S. and European clients make over the years is the assumption that the management practices that served them well in their domestic markets will likewise serve them well in Asia. After all, they are well-seasoned executives with notable track records of success; they are among their firm's best and that is why they have been selected to run the company's international operations. The problem is that those practices are often the only ones they know, and it does not occur to them that other approaches and methods may be necessary. After all, we do not know what we do not know.

As we have seen throughout this book, management in Asia and in the West is profoundly different. The road to succeeding in managing in Asia is quite a different road than the one that successful Western companies have traveled down in their domestic markets. The speed limits that are observed on the road of management are very different—faster in America and Europe, much slower in Asia. The road contours are likewise dissimilar—straight and direct in the West with our linear logic and straightforward approach versus winding and rambling in Asia where a holistic mindset requires taking an integrated view along the scenic route the parties need to travel as they incorporate not only the specifics of their shared business project but also the varied and complex requirements of broader mutual interests and relationship.

As the roads of successful managing are different in these two geographic areas, a map for successfully managing in a Western nation is often not an effective guide to managing in Asia.

Would anyone expect a road map of New York City to be effective in getting them where they want to go in Singapore, Shanghai, or Seoul? In the same way, we cannot assume that the practices of Western management will produce optimal results when brought to Asia. Consequently, it is highly advisable that Western executives initially neither pack nor bring with them to international markets the management practices used in their home market.

Western companies would be better served starting out with the stance that customary management practices used in their home market will not be effective in a foreign market. Management should instead use firsthand experience, market research, input from local market experts such as their local managers, their in-house facilitator interpreter, peers, and consultants to gain a better understanding of the management practices of that market and what that means for achieving their business objectives. Doing so will allow them to confirm what in their previous experiences can be successfully utilized in each individual global market and what modifications are required. This mindset is one of the most important pieces of luggage you *should* pack and bring along on your international management journey.

II. THE RIGHT PRODUCTS FOR ASIAN MARKETS

It is common for businesses to adopt a cookie-cutter approach regarding which products to sell when expanding into foreign markets. That one-size-fits-all approach, however, is often not effective. For example, executives tend to think that their current best-selling product in their domestic market will be a best seller in each international market. While this can be true some of the time, it is not true all the time. In my experience, it is not uncommon for a client's best-selling product in the U.S. or Europe to fail to achieve the same status in Asia—indeed, sometimes that product hardly sold at all.

Which, then, of its many products should a company select in order to achieve the best possible sales results as it expands into international markets? This is a critical decision that needs to be carefully considered as executives formulate both their market entry and long-term business strategies for each country. There are several market conditions and management considerations that should go into determining which products to sell in each individual market. These include the following specific factors:

A. MANAGING INTERNATIONAL REGULATORY REGIMES

The time and cost for applying for regulatory approval from Asian governments to import and sell foreign products varies from country to country and industry to industry from a few months to several years and from a few thousand dollars to several million dollars. The time to clarify the regulatory circumstances of products and decide on an optimal regulatory strategy is early in the planning stage of market entry. A well-qualified potential local partner in each country or an industry consultant will be able to assist with this.

> Failure to effectively manage a target market's regulatory issues early on can cost international companies years of time and millions of dollars in unnecessary expenses.

Failure to effectively manage a target market's regulatory issues early on can cost international companies years of time and millions of dollars in unnecessary expenses. Regulatory considerations should be among the first items Western executives take care of—this point cannot be emphasized enough. If a potential local partner is not effective in your efforts to determine your firm's regulatory strategy in their market that is a definite red flag; it is an indication that they are not an appropriate partner, and you should seek an alternative one. Criteria for selecting your local partner will be discussed later in this chapter.

An additional concern is that regulatory approval may require product redesign, reformulation, or reconstitution. Such changes may have a negative impact on the product's performance, effectiveness, and price or even result in a completely different product that may or may not meet market expectations.

There are instances where a best-selling product might require considerably more time and cost to earn approval than a company's less popular product. Executives need to weigh whether it makes sense to start with those secondary products while the company's best-selling products are still undergoing government approval for sale in the future.

A regulatory review of a company's best-selling product may even determine that the product cannot be sold in an international market due to prohibitive redevelopment costs, time-to-market delays, or because so many product alterations would be needed to meet government requirements that the product would no longer be able to provide its original performance or benefits.

B. MARKET DEMAND FOR MULTIPLE PRODUCT CATEGORIES

When Western manufacturers have more than one product category, demand for their best-selling product category may not necessarily be as strong in Asian countries as in other markets. There are occasions when one of a firm's secondary product categories experiences greater demand there than its primary product category. In that case, executives need to decide whether it would make sense to make that secondary product category the main products in those markets and consider how that would impact the company's global positioning and brand management strategy.

C. SELECTING PRODUCTS FROM WITHIN THE BEST-SELLING CATEGORY

It is common for Western companies to research the competitive standing of their best-selling products abroad to understand how those products might fare in international markets. However, rather than taking it for granted that those leading products in its best-selling category will be the company's best performers overseas, the company should analyze their other products in that same best-selling product category to see how they fare. It could turn out that a lower or even much lower ranking product in one's domestic market is a more appealing product abroad than a best-selling product.

It could turn out that a lower ranking product in one's domestic market is a more appealing product abroad than a best-selling product.

In the experience of one client, the manufacturer of the leading dermatological laser in the U.S., their best-selling laser turned out to be too large for the much smaller operating rooms and clinics typical in their target Asian markets. However, the much smaller and portable demo unit used to demonstrate the lasers across the country was appropriately scaled. While not offering the full range of capabilities as the full-sized product, the demo unit version still incorporated the company's unique technology and enough advantages over competing products in the market that it became the company's best-selling product in Asia's largest dermatological laser markets.

D. STRENGTHS OF YOUR ASIAN PARTNER

Within each international market, potential business partners will have their own different strengths and weaknesses. Western executives need to carefully analyze both when assessing potential partner companies. It can be anticipated that any given company is better suited to sell certain of your company's total product line than others. This is due to several factors including the following:

- The Asian company's resources
- Their standing in their respective industry
- Their strength in their specific product categories
- Their strength in each of the sales channels your products have the potential to be sold in
- The degree of their nationwide distribution and sales capability

- The geographic appropriateness of their nationwide distribution and sales capability for your specific products—specifically, whether their customer base represents the largest and most appropriate group of potential users for your products in that market

- The company's ability to collaborate with top-ranked product spokespersons when appropriate for your products

As a result, partner selection also impacts which products make sense to focus on in each market. There are occasions where those products are not the ones executives originally had planned for each international market.

E. INFLUENCE OF SALES CHANNELS

Like most major markets, Asian countries have numerous major sales channels, including the following:

- Traditional wholesale and retail channels
- E-commerce
- Discount sales channel
- Professional use product channels such as healthcare
- Direct marketing sales channel
- Television shopping
- Network marketing (multilevel marketing)

Product sales volumes vary depending on the sales channels in which they are sold. Products may end up needing to be sold in one channel as opposed to another as a result of the partner company's preference, regulatory guidelines, market requirements, pricing, or experience of the Asian firm. These factors will greatly influence sales channel strategy as well as product selection and promotion strategies.

> Succeeding in sales channels with lower sales volume potential can yield greater total sales volume in the long term.

In the event a Western company's products can be sold in more than one sales channel, its executives may not want to automatically select the channel likely to result in the greatest sales volume at the outset. Succeeding in certain sales channels with lower sales volume potential initially can yield greater total sales volume in the long term by establishing your company's corporate identity, brand image, and market leadership in the local market. Once established, these strengths can be transferred to other sales channels resulting in greater sales volumes than otherwise would have been possible.

For example, if products can be sold in both the medical and retail channels, it is usually better to commence sales in the medical channel even though it is expected to have smaller sales volume potential. Why? Success in the medical channel establishes a higher level of credibility for a company, its brand, and its product than can be attained in retail channels. Once branding and credibility are attained in the medical channel that credibility and market leadership can be transferred to other sales channels, typically resulting in even greater sales volume than would have been possible entering those non-medical sales channels first. With appropriate products, this approach strengthens a Western company's market share not only in the short term but over the long term as well. We previously discussed the importance of American and European companies demonstrating to their Asian counterparts that they are committed to the Asian market for the long term; approaching markets with this strategy is another concrete way Western executives can do so.

Conversely, products that succeed in the retail channel first and then are launched in the medical channel generally do not do as well in either channel. The primary reason for this is that physicians are skeptical of the clinical efficacy of products that become popular as retail products first. Products categorized as medical products require a manufacturer to provide proof of a significantly greater level of clinical results than is necessary for retail channel products. Therefore, the clinical efficacy of products made by retail product makers is often questioned by physicians and consumers.

F. CONSUMER PREFERENCES

In addition to regulatory requirements, Western products often need to be modified to meet consumer preferences in Asian markets. Two representative product preference examples include:

- **Product size** – Different markets prefer different sizes of the same products. In the U.S., we tend to like bigger products, where the option to supersize an order is ubiquitous. This is not the case in Asia. The Japanese market, for example, is at the other end of the preferred-size spectrum, requiring products that are sized smaller than in most other countries.

- **Product features** – Consumer expectations and demands for a product's performance will dictate what features a product must have. As is true in any international market, products must meet the specific market needs of each individual Asian country if they are to sell well there.

G. NUMBER OF PRODUCTS — THE SHARPSHOOTER VS. SHOTGUN APPROACH

In the event your company has a large product line, it is advisable to enter international markets with a select few products initially rather than many of or the entire product line at once, and then add more products over time. Taking this sharpshooter rather than shotgun approach to launching products allows Western firms and their Asian partners to focus on, monitor, manage, and maximize product sales with greater efficiency and effectiveness.

This sharpshooter product selection approach generally yields yet another important benefit. Launching in Asian markets with fewer rather than a greater number of product SKUs and then adding products as the first products become established usually results in greater success in establishing an international company's market share and brand leadership.

H. CULTURAL TRANSLATABILITY

In order to succeed in an international market, the names of your company and its products need to translate well culturally in that foreign market. Likewise, any marketing slogans need to be checked for cultural appropriateness and effectiveness.

To cite a few examples:

- When the company Best Buy entered the China market, its name was translated into Chinese as *bai si mai* (百思买). Meaning "to buy after thinking 100 times," this name tells potential customers that they must work very hard to decide what to buy from that store—not the most effective name to attract customers.

- The initial Chinese rendition of Kentucky Fried Chicken's famous "Finger-lickin' good" marketing slogan was "Eat your fingers off."

- The first translation of Coca-Cola in Chinese (*ke-kou-kela)* meant "bite the wax tadpole."

- Coca-Cola's arch rival Pepsi Cola did not fare any better; the translation in Taiwan for its early slogan "Come alive with the Pepsi Generation" meant "Pepsi will bring our ancestors back from the dead."

- Clairol, the popular hair care products manufacturer, sold their "Mist Stick" curling iron in Germany without realizing that in German slang the word "mist" means manure.

- When Schweppes Tonic Water was first introduced into the Italian market, the Italian translation meant Schweppes Toilet Water. Italians certainly do not desire to drink toilet water. An additional point of market confusion: Since "toilet water" typically refers to a light perfume, was the product tonic water or a perfume?

This cultural translatability problem of company and product names is huge and has the potential to limit success potential in international markets.

Foreign companies entering the American market are not immune from the same problem. Electrolux, the Scandinavian maker of vacuum cleaners, launched their business in the States with the marketing slogan "Nothing sucks like an Electrolux." When Japan's top-tier Otsuka Pharmaceutical Company launched "Calpis," a block buster sports drink in their domestic market, in the U.S., its name was adopted and pronounced as "cow piss." Is it any wonder that sales of these products suffered greatly due to ineffective intercultural management until they were remedied?

The problem of cultural translatability does not apply only to the names of companies and products. The names of company executives can likewise have undesirable meanings, as discussed later in this chapter.

> General Motors Corporation has made over six hundred product alterations to their Buick Century model car since launching it in China.

Adapting products in order to maximize one's success in international markets can be a daunting task. International executives may think that product adaptation occurs only during the initial stage of entering foreign markets. This, however, is often not the case. The General Motors Corporation, for example, has made over six hundred product alterations to their Buick Century model car since launching it in China in 1998 in order to meet the evolving requirements and preferences of that market.[20]

III. SELECTING THE RIGHT INTERNATIONAL PARTNERS

A. SCREENING AND SELECTING THE RIGHT PARTNER

When international companies seek to enter a foreign market, there are often several potential partners that they will meet with to screen and make their partner selection. How can they most effectively screen, evaluate, and select the most appropriate local business partner in Asian markets, and what criteria should international executives use in doing so? I have developed the following fifteen major criteria that have served my clients well:

(1) **The history of the Asian company:** It is important to research the company's track record. How long has the company been in business and how successful have they been in meeting their goals?

(2) **Experience and capabilities:** Regardless of how long a company has been operating and how successful they may be overall, it is necessary to study the company's length, depth, and breadth of experience in *your* firm's particular industry, desired sales channel, and product category. For example, one former client was interested in partnering with a major Beijing-based corporation that presented themselves as a strong potential partner.

20 Tian, Xiaowen. *Managing International Business in China.* Cambridge, UK: Cambridge University Press, 2016. Page 21

My client's director of international sales had met with that company and wanted to select them as their partner. However, in conducting due diligence for my client after that, I discovered that the company became large and successful by manufacturing industrial batteries and had no experience or inroads in my client's industry or product segment. It became clear that the Chinese company's interest was to use my client's business as the opportunity to enter my client's industry and benefit from the prestige of my client's reputation.

It is important to determine a potential partner's actual capabilities and possible weaknesses related to your specific business goals and needs. For example, does the company sell directly to the end-users of your product or do they need to go through intermediaries? Obviously, selling directly to product end-users is most favorable. Depending on the particulars, an Asian company's selling to end-users through one intermediary sales company can be unproblematic, but generally speaking, a potential partner company's need for multiple intermediaries is not desirable and should be viewed as a potential red flag warranting sufficient investigation.

(3) **Financial performance:** What is the company's overall financial condition? Review the company's track record for sales and profitability over the past five and ten years as well as their projections for the next five and ten years. Remember, Asian companies are accustomed to such a long-term management horizon.

(4) **Corporate culture and management strategy:** Within any industry, every company has its own corporate culture, management approach, and strategic objectives. Western executives should determine to what degree the prospective partner's culture, approach, and strategy align with their own.

For instance, if a European company's strategic objectives for an international market include high priority for establishing the company, brand, and product as an industry leader there, is the potential partner likewise interested in that goal? Is the potential partner experienced in achieving that goal? Or, in contrast, are they a "flavor of the month" type of company solely interested in selling as many units of your product for as long as sales are strong, but then moving on to other business projects? Even more problematic, does their history and reputation indicate that they are willing to "push the envelope" and engage in actions that are gray area activities, outright questionable, or that skirt existing or expected laws and regulations governing your industry, product, or trademarks?

(5) **Industry standing:** Whenever possible, seek out top tier prospects for potential partnerships. What is the company's standing in their industry? Obviously, the greater a company's standing in their industry, the more they are likely to be able to bring to your business and, consequently, the stronger a partner they are likely to be. While there sometimes are exceptions, as a general rule, it is not advisable to work with a company that is not in the top tier of their industry.

The Korean market presents an interesting situation in this regard. Despite the fact that eighty percent of Korea's economy is dominated by its four major conglomerates, there are many industries in which the only companies are small and mid-sized firms. One example is the medical skin care industry. It is noteworthy that when these smaller companies present themselves to Western companies seeking business in Korea, they all claim to be number one in their industry. According to them, there is no number two or three. Every Korean company that approaches an international company states that it is number one in their domestic industry! That math obviously does not add up, which is why Western executives need to properly investigate prospective partner companies before selecting them.

(6) **Industry reputation:** While industry standing is a measurable level of a company's achievement for things such as sales revenues or market share, industry reputation is how a company is perceived and thought of by others in the industry and society at large. For example, how is the company regarded by fellow professionals in that industry? Does the company have a reputation for conducting business in a professional, legal, and ethical manner or are they known for cutting corners, engaging in questionable business practices, or stealing the intellectual property of foreign firms?

(7) **Spokesperson collaboration:** In the event that sales of your company's products can be enhanced by utilizing a spokesperson such as a celebrity, physician, or sports player, you need to ascertain if a potential international partner has a track record of attracting and working with the right spokespersons.

If the leading spokespersons in your industry in an Asian market do not work with a company that is interested in your business, that is definitely a red flag. Likewise, the caliber of the spokespersons who do work with the partner company is indicative of that company's standing and reputation in their market. For example, if a company's spokesperson for a medical product is not a first tier, recognized authority physician, it is advisable to remove that company from partner consideration.

(8) **Sufficient financial resources:** A potential international partner company should possess sufficient financial

resources to market, sell, and provide after-sales customer care and maintenance to the level required to succeed in the foreign market. Equally important to *possessing* sufficient financial resources, are they *committing* the requisite resources—financial and other?

(9) **Appropriate sales plan:** Consider how likely a potential partner's business plans are to attain your desired goals for their market. Are their plans likely to achieve your expected level of sales and to advance your standing and reputation in the international market? Furthermore, does the company have successful experience executing the sales activities included in its business plan for your company? Western firms can access this information from industry insiders, consultants, market research firms, and government agencies.

While capital is a major factor, it is not the only commitment factor to consider when assessing a potential partner company's commitment to your business.

(10) **Corporate commitment:** While capital is a major factor, it is not the only commitment factor to consider when assessing a potential partner company's commitment to your business. A more complete list would include:

- Number of employees they are committing to the business.
- Number of company departments or divisions that will be involved.
- Number of affiliates in the case of large corporations; in the case of small and medium-sized firms, the number of collaborating companies.

- Number of years of the company's plan for the business project included *within* your business agreement with them: Two years? Three years? Five years?

- As we have discussed, Asian companies engage in business with a long-term orientation. Accordingly, a top-tier company will have a plan for your business for *beyond* the time period specified in most business agreements. Discussing this with a potential partner company provides Western executives with a much clearer understanding of the local company's level of interest and commitment.

(11) **Exclusive or non-exclusive business agreement:** A foreign company's insistence on having exclusive rights in its business agreement with your company is a major indicator of how serious their interest is. A major industry player and strong candidate partner company always will insist on exclusive rights. If they are going to make a major commitment to a business project, they want to make sure their company reaps the benefits and not their competitors. If they do not clamor for exclusive rights, that is a major red flag, and international executives should remove that company from consideration.

(12) **Project launch:** The scale of the project launch the potential Asian partner is proposing to officially commence the business in their market reflects their commitment, financial involvement, and corporate capabilities. Examine where the company proposes to conduct the launch, whom they are planning to invite, and the scale of the event.

For example, is it a ninety-minute ceremony inside their

company and only employees are invited? Is it a half-day affair that takes place in the grand ballroom of one of the major hotels in the capital of their country with leaders from government, business, the media, and the community invited and involved? Furthermore, will they have only one launch program or will they hold launch events in several major cities? The greater the project launch planned, the greater their interest, commitment, and expectations are for the business.

(13) **Manufacturer or sales company:** It is important to know if the prospective partner is a manufacturer or if they are a sales company only. With potential partner companies that are manufacturers, there is always the inherent risk that they will incorporate knowledge of your products into their own product line and eventually produce or sell products that will compete—if not directly then indirectly through affiliates or companies where they have "cooperative relationships." Companies that are sales companies only are safer in that regard.

(14) **Banks:** In many Asian markets, company profiles list the banks that a company does business with. The rank and status of those banks is indicative of the company's financial strength and reputation in their domestic market. A country's better banks work with their country's better companies. So, if money-center banks in an Asian country do not collaborate with a local company, Western executives should be cautious in partnering with them.

(15) **Motivation:** Potential partner companies in international markets have any number of motivations for wanting to work with a Western company in their domestic market, including gaining the opportunity to work with a leading foreign company to enlarge their market share, expand sales and profit,

and increase their standing in their domestic industry. These, of course, are desirable motivations international executives seek in partner companies. However, there are several other reasons why companies in foreign markets want to work with Western firms and those reasons are not at all in the Western company's interests. The following are some of the more noteworthy reasons I have seen at play:

> Potential partner companies in international markets have any number of motivations for wanting to work with a Western company and not all those reasons are in the Western company's interests.

- Obtaining and benefiting from the proprietary knowhow or intellectual property belonging to a Western company

- Securing a business agreement with a prominent U.S. or European company as a source of great pride

  Becoming the partner of a leading foreign company provides a local company with bragging rights among their peers in their domestic industry. I call these "trophy rights" since the company is motivated more by the prestige of saying they are working with such and such a foreign company than in actually developing the business. Such companies collect business agreements on their mantel as if they were trophies.

- Securing the business rights to a well-known

international company's products to help establish their company as the market leader among their domestic competitors

- Tying up the foreign company to *keep it out* of the international market

  In these cases, the local company is planning on launching or is already selling a similar product line either themselves or through a related company, so they drag their feet during the negotiations, during the process to obtain government approval to import and sell your product, and during the roll out and sales of the product. The international partner engages in minimal marketing and sales efforts on behalf of the Western firm's product. Western companies can lose several years of investment, opportunity, market share, and profit as a result.

Clearly these four motivations are not in the interests of Western companies. International executives need to be extra diligent in ascertaining the interests of companies they are screening. Industry insiders, consultants, lawyers, and other industry experts are in a position to assist with this.

Partner selection is perhaps the most important decision Western executives must make in commencing business internationally. As negotiating provides the initial and critically important opportunity to screen and select a partner, Western companies should use that opportunity to do so wisely. When international companies work with the wrong partner company, they can pay a huge cost in terms of time, capital, energy, corporate image, product reputation, competitiveness, momentum, and lost sales and profit. In Asian markets, there is one additional negative consequence of selecting the wrong partner.

Generally speaking, Asian companies do not look favorably on foreign companies changing business partners there. In their view, changing business partners means a relationship breakdown occurred and that indicates the foreign company did not appropriately value and manage the relationship with its local partner. Consequently, foreign companies need to make careful decisions to get it right the first time when selecting their international business partners.

B. SEEK A STRATEGIC PARTNER, NOT A DISTRIBUTOR

Western companies generally frame their search for a company to work with in a foreign market in terms of finding a good sales company or distributor there. However, that is often a strategic misstep as maximum success is achieved by working with a strategic partner rather than a distributor in international markets.

Maximum success is achieved by working with a strategic partner rather than a distributor in international markets.

What is the difference between a distributor and a strategic partner? A distributor is solely interested in selling as many units of a given product as possible during the life of the sales cycle. When sales wane, so does distributor interest and effort toward marketing your product. While product sales represent the entirety of interest for a distributor, sales are but one part of the interest of a strategic partner.

Product sales are equally significant to a partner; however, a partner views your business as an integral part of their own business. They see your business as being an important part of their overall corporate strategy and, as a result, focus on the strategic dimensions of what is needed to maximize your company's success in their market. That includes establishing your company's corporate image, company brand, unique technology, and product line as a leader in its industry segment for the long term. And they are willing and able to make the requisite investments needed to do so. This provides buoyancy for the longevity of your business in that market; if there is a sales slowdown, for example, strategic interest and relational merit keep a partner focused on the business project while a distributor will have moved on.

This is a powerful difference between a partner and a distributor in international markets and the significant benefit that a partner brings to Western executives. In addition, this dynamic further illustrates fundamental role of relationship in Asian markets. While relationship building and management may cost American and European companies additional time and effort, the business payoffs are tangible and generally well worth the investment.

The following are additional major benefits that a strategic partner provides to an international company that a distributor does not:

- Your company's success in their market is a major priority for a partner company. This is evidenced in

  - The number and quality of management and staff they assign to your project.
  - The amount of capital they commit to promoting your business.
  - The level and frequency of promotional activities they engage in for your project.

- A partner ensures that your product and its underlying concept are properly understood in the market. They achieve that objective by engaging in appropriate marketing and educational activities on a regular basis throughout the market, including product usage workshops designed for those selling the products, providing product maintenance, and for end-users.

- A partner respects and vigorously helps you defend your intellectual property. That means they take the lead in identifying and going after companies that infringe on your intellectual property.

- A partner actively updates you on competitive developments in their market that impact your business and proactively seeks new strategies and solutions to best deal with them in real time.

- A partner will go out of their way to find suggestions for you to improve your product so it can have greater appeal—and sales—in their market.

When a U.S. or European company selects a distributor to work with in an international market, it is equivalent to the Western firm starting their business there in the batter's box trying to get a hit and advance to first base. When a Western company has a strategic partner that is fully committed to going to bat for them, the Western firm starts its business there on second base.

I strongly recommend that international executives take advantage of the traits of a partner company and the requirements of Asia's business culture to advance their corporate interests by working with a full-fledged strategic partner and not just a distributor. By being aware of and strategically navigating Asia's divergent management practices, Western executives can better ensure that their success in Asian markets is both optimal and long term.

IV. THE RIGHT EMPLOYEES FOR INTERNATIONAL MARKETS

Another often overlooked business consideration management needs to be fully cognizant of and effectively prepare for is having the most appropriate employees representing their company in international markets. Simply put, not every employee will be effective in working in international markets. Having the right members on the company's international team is critical; it will directly impact just about every facet of your business there including:

- How smoothly initial discussions and negotiations proceed.
- How productive the company's communication and relationship ends up being with the international partner.

- How strong and long term the international partner's commitment to the business is.

- Whether a company achieves maximum success, moderate success, minimal success, or outright fails in international markets.

What are the right types of employees that companies need to have on their international teams? Contrary to what Western executives often believe, the employees who get the best results in foreign markets are not necessarily the company's best domestic market performers. In fact, the best performing employees domestically can turn out to be the ones who have the hardest time in Asia and become an obstacle to the business interests of Western companies there. The reason is that their domestic market success often acts as blinders that make it difficult to recognize, acknowledge, and navigate Asia's different management fundamentals.

The ideal candidates for a company's international team have specific characteristics. They are aware of—and accepting of—other cultures. They are flexible. They realize that there is more than one way to engage in a task or achieve a goal. While they possess confidence, they are not insistent on their own way of doing things but rather are patient with and open-minded regarding indigenous approaches to conducting business. They realize that just as there is more than one train to take them to a destination, there can be more than one way things are done in any given market. The proverbial bull in the china shop is precisely the person you do *not* want involved in your international business, regardless of how successful they may be domestically.

At least one member of your international team needs

to be experienced in the local market of interest. If a potential member of your international team has had previous experience working there, make sure that experience is not out of date. I have worked with clients who hired such professionals and witnessed numerous times how their way of conducting business was not only unsuccessful but even detrimental. Experience needs to be qualified in terms of how recent, relevant, and strong it is relative to your company's specific needs, objectives, and long-term strategic goals.

As discussed in chapter nine, your company needs to have your own *facilitator interpreter* on your team to provide accurate cultural interpretation, linguistic translation, market analysis, and management practice adaptation. This person can advance corporate goals and business interests by bridging the differences in management fundamentals and business practices between one's domestic and foreign markets. He or she can ensure that your company successfully navigates culture-based differences in management practices and the market so that instead of those differences hindering your firm's results, those differences can be intentionally and strategically leveraged to enhance your success in international markets.

Having a facilitator interpreter on your team is comparable to having both the correct address in the target Asian market and a GPS system to take you where you want to go; the company knows its destination and has the right tools to get it there without ending up getting lost, taking detours, going down dead-end streets, or having misspent time and expenses. Executives who do not have these assets on their company team only have an address; they may know *where* they want to go in an international market in terms of objectives but have no idea *how* to get there and are quite often unaware of the obstacles and pitfalls that await along the way.

I have always found Asian markets to be very unforgiving; businesses are expected to get it right the first time. So, it is important that Western companies select the right people to represent them from the outset in any international market, have a business plan that is appropriate for each specific market, and possess management strategies that take into account the actual realities of the target market.

This is especially true in Asia where relationship requirements and expectations present an additional level of challenge that is not present in the U.S. and Europe. Changing members of one's on-site management team in Asia is often not viewed favorably. In day-to-day management, it is considered disruptive to the smooth operations of your joint business. In negotiating and planning, it is thought of as interfering with the flow and momentum of the discussions. This is especially true in China where negotiating occurs more on a person-to-person level than a company-to-company level. Given this negotiating dynamic in China, personnel changes are seen as an opportunity to revisit previously negotiated items that did not turn out quite the way the Chinese company had hoped. A new negotiator representing a Western company is viewed by Chinese negotiators as a new opportunity to renegotiate what they want, as the new person might be more amenable to the Chinese position.

Another consideration is that seniority and rank are very important in Asian countries. It would create a negative perception if a low or middle-level manager was sent to represent your company there. Asian executives generally react by feeling insulted and assume that the Western company is not serious about the business project. Make sure you know the rank of the highest-level executive at the Asian company who will be in the meeting and that your highest-ranking company representative is a comparable level executive.

Last, it is highly advisable to determine how the names of your company executives representing your business interests translate into the language of each international market.

To share a client example, the name of the international sales director was Joe Dunn. While a name common in the States, in Japanese that name has the same pronunciation as the word for "joke"—*jou-dan* (冗談). Japanese executives would often be embarrassed as they sought not to chuckle upon hearing his name for the first time and would inevitably joke about it later. A Western company being represented by a senior executive—in this case, its international sales director—who introduces himself by saying "Hello, I am a joke" is clearly not the ideal posture or image you want your company to project when trying to succeed in international markets that are as highly competitive and nuanced as Asia.

V. INTERNAL ORGANIZATIONAL IMPEDIMENTS TO SUCCESS

As a management consultant, I have always been amazed at how successful companies can be in spite of themselves. Despite ineffective management, inefficiencies, poor performance, and other self-created obstacles impeding optimal success, better companies tend to continue doing well.

Still, organizational impediments in management are factors that curtail success. Differing from company to company and being too numerous to cover here, the purpose of this section is to alert the reader to their existence and hopefully prompt executives to review their own businesses to identify and eliminate them as part of their preparation for managing and maximizing business interests in international markets.

The following are some of the more common organizational impediments in international management that I have come across:

- The management goals set for the new market are not fully in line with the company's overall strategic interests. Even when successful, that very success causes the company problems in the areas where the underlying goals are incongruous with the firm's broader strategic interests.

- Poor communication, competition, or rivalry among the company's departments results in the company internationalizing its business without the proper and complete involvement of all relevant departments—the vertical and horizontal alignment of management discussed in chapter two. This results in problems and inefficiencies when it is time to implement the operation.

- Personal ambition of the heads of the departments involved in managing international operations can hinder progress. Specifically, a department manager puts their departmental or personal concerns above the overall interests of the organization.

- Insufficient knowledge of and/or experience in the target market regarding one's business, industry conditions, regulatory requirements, economic conditions, potential foreign partners, and management fundamentals always impede progress.

- The outlook of company executives is not conducive to optimizing success in international business. Walmart executives, for instance, when interviewed by Forbes India and asked to describe their company's global mindset, described it as follows: "Our global mindset is below zero — we are a US company doing business abroad and not a global company." [21]

- A firm's internal corporate culture is not conducive to effectively dealing with the cultural differences that govern the divergent needs and management practices of the international market, leaving them unable to correctly understand and deal with obstacles to success.

- Management lacks the interest or staying power to meet the long-term commitment and investment required in many international markets. This is especially true with Asian markets.

Each of these is a critically important facet of managing in international markets. Failing to address them will invariably have high costs in terms of time, effort, capital, resources, company reputation, brand image, and bottom-line results.

21 Accessed December 5, 2021. https://www.forbesindia.com/article/big-bet/walmarts-passage-to-india/6002/1.

VI. SIX MARKET DETERMINANTS OF MANAGEMENT PRACTICE TYPES

Far from uniform, individual markets in Asia and their business practices over time vary in terms of the degree to which they align more with indigenous versus international management practices. Furthermore, within each individual country the type of management practices at work will vary from industry to industry, company to company, and individual to individual.

On one end of the management practices spectrum, there are companies that utilize indigenous methods based on traditional cultural values and social expectations, such as those highlighted throughout this book. On the other end of the spectrum, internationally accepted business practices govern in other companies. The factors determining the type of management practices international executives find in each country—that is, the degree management practices are more indigenous or more Western—depends on several factors, including the following:

- The level of economic development and international business interaction of the nation
- The degree of maturity of the industry a company is in
- The degree of success of a specific company within its industry
- The degree of experience with international business of a specific company

- The degree of experience, success, and comfort with international business on the part of the individual executives involved

- The degree to which the rule of Western law is established and practiced[22]

In my experience, the management practices one encounters in international markets depend on the status of these six factors. The weaker these factors are, the more indigenous the management practices utilized typically are. Conversely, the greater these factors are, the more commonly accepted international management practices are found. The following figure illustrates this dynamic.

Figure 11: Determinants of the Prevalence of Indigenous vs. International Management Practices

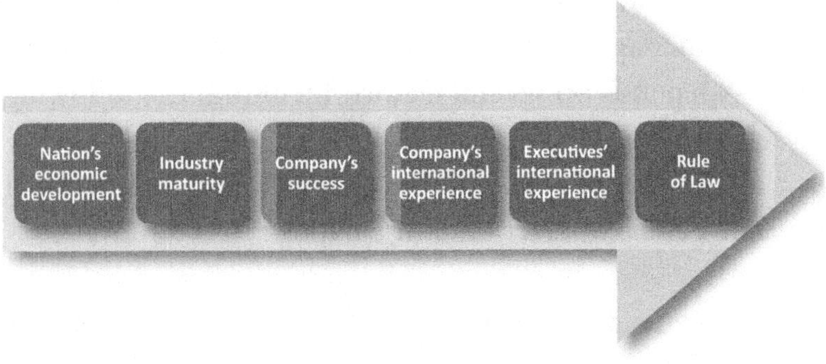

Source: Robert Charles Azar, 2021

The level of indigenous as opposed to international management practices varies from country to country based on these factors. For example, management practices in Singapore are

22 The World Justice Project Rule of Law Index is a leading source of global rankings of the rule of law. See Appendix 1 of this book and https://worldjusticeproject.org.

generally more international in nature than those in China, Japan, Korea, Thailand, Indonesia, or Vietnam.

In addition, within each individual nation, the type of management practices will differ across industries according to these factors. For instance, a country's IT industry typically employs more international management practices than its textile or agriculture industry.

Likewise, even in the same industry in a given market, the management practices in each company will vary based on these factors. Generally, the more experience and success a firm has outside of its domestic market, the more international its management practices tend to become over time.

In addition, the management practices utilized within the same corporation will vary depending on each individual manager in charge. For instance, the initial executive of an Asian partner company that a Western firm interacts with may be quite international in their approach to business and management practices. However, a subsequent manager may be more traditional in their outlook and less comfortable or open to international management practices or even to working with international partners—a problematic situation I witnessed my clients struggle with on numerous occasions throughout the region.

The degree to which the rule of Western law is established in each country is a salient factor impacting the type of management found in international markets. First, the ability of Western companies to obtain a fair and meaningful resolution to commercial disputes will be determined in large part by how well accepted and practiced Western law is in each foreign market. Second, the greater the degree to which Western law governs commercial activity, the greater the respect for and protection of Western companies' intellectual property is likely to be. In short, a greater prevalence of the rule of Western law is generally commensurate with a greater degree of international management practices. Conversely, markets that utilize traditional rules and expectations in business tend to be characterized by more indigenous management practices.

As a result of these six major factors, the landscape of management practices found in international business is diverse, multi-dimensional, and dynamic; these factors are not static, but rather change over time, and as they do, so too do the management practices of international markets and partners around the world. The more international executives familiarize themselves with these factors and the impact their interplay has on international management, the more adept they will be at accurately understanding and navigating the different and diverse management practices they encounter as they develop their business in each unique international market.

Regarding intellectual property, international executives will also find that observance of intellectual property rights is commensurate with the level of economic development of a nation. In the early stages of economic development, the primary focus of companies is catching up with industrialized nations, and rules do not receive priority attention. It is only as countries advance economically that international rules are given more credence. When a nation begins to industrialize, its companies have nothing to lose in terms of intellectual property. It is only as they advance and develop their own intellectual property that they have for the first time something to lose and therefore tout protecting intellectual property rights.

Chapter 6

PRACTICAL MANAGEMENT PROTOCOLS FOR ASIA

Man's common nature brings people together, while differences in customs and practices keep them apart. —**Confucius**

I. APPROPRIATE DISCUSSION VENUE AND COMMUNICATION DYNAMICS

In part due to the prominence of relationship in business, Asian companies often prefer face-to-face meetings rather than electronic or telephone communication. This is especially true for discussions of substantive matters. In the case of strategic management issues, for example, face-to-face communication is expected.

Western executives generally place high priority on

> Taking the time, expense, and effort to travel in order to meet face-to-face is a measure of a company's level of interest and commitment.

expediency and convenience, so they are comfortable communicating via email and even using email in major discussions regarding negotiating, planning, and strategy execution. Asian counterparts, in contrast, see taking the time, expense, and effort to travel in order to meet face-to-face as a reflection of how important the matter is to the parties as well as a measure of a company's level of interest and commitment.

Typically, the frequency of face-to-face discussion is the greatest during the early stages of collaboration starting with the "becoming acquainted" stage and on through the negotiation process, the signing of the business agreement, the official launch of the project, the roll-out phase, and the early stages of the business. After that, the frequency of face-to-face meetings tends to decrease though they still remain an essential part of maintaining both your business interest and your relationship with your Asian partner. This is true for as long as you engage in business in the region.

After companies commence working together, have established a strong rapport, and have built a successful track record, Asian executives then have a sufficient comfort level to utilize indirect communication to a greater degree. Younger and more internationally minded managers tend to be the first in their companies to engage in this shift. However, it is worth reiterating that while companies are in the early stages of relationship building and collaboration, substantive communication commonly occurs in person.

Asian executives will continue to require face-to-face communication even after a strong working relationship has been established in the event of major developments, including problems related to regulatory issues, consumer use, conflicts with third parties, and new product launches.

There are other times when proactively initiating face-to-face meetings is highly recommended after project commencement:

- **Sales training for your Asian business partner:** Sales training will be needed both before and after launching your business in Asia. Any foreign company seeking to maximize its success in Asian markets should plan to provide training on new product developments and sales on a regular basis for the duration of its business efforts there. The more you keep your partner company focused on selling your products, the more they will keep their salespeople and marketing efforts focused on selling your products.

- **Product usage training for product retailers and users:** For example, you sell medical products to your Asian partner (your wholesale customer) who, in turn, sells your products to hospitals or clinics (retailers). The clinic then uses your product to treat their patients (product users). The training for your retailers (hospitals, clinics, etc.) and product users needs to be done jointly by your company and your Asian sales partner. The greater the frequency, typically the greater your success. This is an additional way you can proactively drive your company's success in each market.

It is noteworthy that in Asian business, these types of sales and product trainings are often conducted with much greater frequency and for a greater length of time than in the West. The additional benefits for doing face-to-face training, rather than simply providing your business partners with sufficient information about your products or services, are numerous and include:

- Obtaining firsthand, detailed market feedback regarding your products and business directly from business partners, retailers, and product end-users.

- Ensuring that all parties involved in your business are not only *fully* informed but also are *accurately* informed. Rather than relying on others to train and educate those participating in your business, your company doing so directly will result in more effective training outcomes and greater sales and market share over the long term. This becomes more relevant and necessary when companies in addition to your partner are involved in developing your business. While your partner may be well informed, it is critically important that their first level sub-distributors are fully and accurately informed as well as any other related parties such as second level sub-distributors, wholesale companies, retail agents, logistics companies, and product spokespersons.

- Developing good will, demonstrating long-term commitment to the Asian market, your partner and other stakeholders there, and directly contributing to building and sustaining momentum for your business in the market.

- Engaging in marketing events that target prospective clients as well as media representatives.

Initial discussion and negotiation meetings typically take place in Asia or wherever your target market is around the world. Given the time and expense of traveling there, it is reasonable and expected for some of the negotiation meetings and post-negotiation business meetings to take place in your home market at your headquarters. The perfect time for Western executives to suggest that the next meeting be in their country is at the conclusion of a meeting in Asia. Inviting the Asian company face-to-face in real time to meet at your domestic corporate headquarters signals to them that you are serious about wanting to build a strong working relationship and business with them.

> If the Asian company hesitates to come to your home market for meetings, that is a major red flag.

As your company endeavors to engage in business in Asia, it is common for more meetings to take place there than in your domestic market as you will want to make firsthand observations, conduct research, and determine decisions about the local market. This might include such actions as visiting factories, warehouses, distributors, retail sales channels, and industry trade shows. During the negotiation process, however, if the Asian company hesitates or does not agree to your invitation to come to your home market for meetings, that is a major red flag. It is a clear sign that their interest in working with your company is weak. It likewise demonstrates an insufficient commitment to your business project. In that case, it would be better to remove them from consideration and seek another business partner for that market.

U.S. executives often suggest Hawaii as a location for face-to-face meetings with Asian companies as a sensible way to deal with meeting venue. While Hawaii is a convenient midpoint location for U.S.-Asian meetings, having negotiating meetings there does not carry the same significance as meeting at your company's corporate headquarters.

Should your U.S. company request an initial negotiating meeting in Hawaii and not at your corporate headquarters, Asian executives will interpret this as a weak interest in them as your partner. They will assume you must be having similar discussions with other potential partners and have not yet narrowed the field. Proposing a meeting in the U.S. at any venue other than one of your corporate locations suggests relational distance to a prospective Asian business partner.

When the Asian firm suggests a Hawaii rendezvous instead of initially meeting at your corporate headquarters that likewise is a red flag. They may be more interested in the opportunity to travel to Hawaii to enjoy a few days of sun and golf than in pursuing business with your company.

Where meetings take place has an additional significance in Asia that is not found in the West. Namely, the more important the topic of the discussion, the more "appropriate" the venue must be. The following are common times and places that are appropriate to discuss topics important to you and your Asian partner:

- During official business meetings at the offices or facilities of either company
- A formal meeting room in a hotel

- During a meal at a restaurant, especially when initiated by your Asian counterpart

- In the evening over dinner or drinks

- On the golf course

Places where substantive business subjects should not be discussed include:

- In hallways

- In elevators

- On the street

- In taxis

- In rest rooms

- In the lobby of a hotel or company offices

- While walking

It is important to remember that Asians are much more formal and have a stronger notion of propriety than Westerners tend to have. In their culture, there is an appropriate time, place, and way to conduct meetings and discuss matters—again, the importance of procedure. Abiding by those "appropriate" ways is how respect is shown to the other party and the mutual business. Following the prescribed protocol is another way each party demonstrates its level of interest in the mutual relationship and business. It is how favorable relationships are promoted and professional standards demonstrated. And it is one mechanism for avoiding misunderstanding and friction with Asian partners.

II. COUNTER-PROPOSING AND SAYING NO

In addition to appropriate time and venue for discussions, another fundamental communication dynamic in Asian societies is not only what to say but, more importantly, what *not* to say. In Asian discussions, saying no or directly disagreeing is not typically done, especially in the early stages of a business relationship. There are two major reasons for this.

The first reason is that saying no and directly disagreeing are considered impolite and are related to the broader cultural orientation in Asia of valuing respectful relationships. Asians go to great lengths to avoid being too clear or direct when communicating. Keeping things vague and not saying no prevents parties from having to either agree or disagree and thereby take sides. This helps support and promote smooth collaborative relationships.

Second, saying no or disagreeing directly indicates you are not concerned about your partner's interests. By saying no you are not only rejecting the specific idea proposed but you also are rejecting outright the larger corporate interest your partner is attempting to discuss with you. This makes you appear inflexible and indicates you are not discussing with "sincerity" in the Asian business cultural context—what would be termed as in good faith in Western culture.

How then can Western executives say no or disagree without offending firms in collectivist cultures that avoid saying no directly? In mediating between Asian and Western cultures and languages, I have found two methods that work very well for disagreeing appropriately.

The first option is instead of replying with "no," respond with "That might be difficult." This generally translates well into the local language. While you are not directly saying no, you are saying you are not in a position to agree, at least not at this point in time. With this reply, you do not come across as being inflexible or disinterested in the interests of the other party but neither have you committed to anything. Also, you have left open the possibility that agreement could be possible at a later point.

The second way to indicate politely that your answer is no is to reply with a counterproposal such as "That certainly is one option for achieving that, but would another option be XYZ?" Then go on to describe your counterproposal.

This cultural dynamic of promoting harmonious relationships through vague and non-direct communication carries such importance that Asian cultures have socially acceptable methods to disagree and numerous expressions to convey no. The problem is that most Westerners would not recognize these expressions as disagreement.

Another socially acceptable method to convey dissent is to do so through a trusted third party. Asians may be vague and non-committal during a meeting, or even reply to proposals saying "yes," then have a third party directly convey their non-agreement after the meeting. The use of third parties in business discussions is widespread to avoid direct disagreement or conflict, thereby maintaining positive relations between the principal parties, Asian to Asian as well as Asian to Western.

Western executives, however, often take this communication dynamic to mean that the Asians were not honest. This, however, is not the case. The motivation in using this dynamic is actually to demonstrate respect and signal their continued interest in working with you. While so many communication dynamics are misunderstood as being negative in this way by non-Asian business professionals, in reality those dynamics are positive. The most effective ways I have found for navigating this challenge are presented in chapters eight and nine.

When Asians do dissent face-to-face, a plethora of expressions they can use comes into play. By way of example, in the Japanese language I know of twenty-two ways to say no. Having so many options indicates just how important it is to avoid replying "no" directly and illustrates how many ways communication dynamics specifically accommodate this preference for highly nuanced, relationship-focused communication.

In the ways to disagree you will find not only the word "no" but also the word "yes"!

Thus, it is interesting to note that in the ways to disagree you will find not only the word no but also the word yes! That is correct, the word yes can also mean no. This begs the question for every Western company conducting business in Asian markets: How on track, really, are your understandings with your Asian partners? When they reply "yes," do they really mean yes? Do they mean no? Or do they mean something in between? This communication challenge is analyzed in part three of this book.

What other impact does this communication dynamic have on discussions in Asia?

Western companies almost always rely on their Asian counterparts to provide the translator when meeting. However, this puts U.S. and European firms at a great tactical and strategic disadvantage. Because of Asia's code of respect, foreigners typically only receive polite, literal translations. To understand the cultural—that is, actual—meaning, foreigners must have a translator *on their team* who is in a position to provide accurate cultural interpretation, including being clear when the Asian company is disagreeing with the Western company's position. We will pursue this critically important point in detail in chapter nine.

These types of Asian cultural and communication dynamics easily lead to inaccurate communication and misunderstandings throughout the entire period of working together. Keep in mind that the difference between the literal meaning and the actual meaning is socially sanctioned in Asia. So well established is this communication dynamic that in Japan, for example, it is codified in the ubiquitous notion of *tatemae* (建前) and *honne* (本音)—that is, what is ostensibly the case versus what is the actual situation. This is part of the collectivist society dynamic of following prescribed protocol. This important communication dynamic of *tatemae* and *honne* is examined in chapter eight.

III. INDICATORS OF INTEREST DURING DISCUSSIONS

As we have seen, due to different management practices and communication dynamics, discussions in Asia require a greater amount of time and input than in the U.S. and Europe. How then can Western executives gauge the level of interest their Asian counterparts have in working together during discussions? There are additional actions that are positive interest level indicators, and there are cautionary signs to be mindful of as well. This section sheds light on how foreign executives can identify the level of interest of their Asian counterparts.

A. WHO ATTENDS DISCUSSION MEETINGS

The first indicator Asian companies give of their level of interest in your business is whom they select to represent them in the early discussions and after your business with them starts. Here are five specific indicators that Western executives benefit from paying attention to in this regard:

- **Rank of attendees:** How senior in the company are the participants? High-level executives attending represent a high level of interest. Conversely, junior manager representatives are indicative of weaker or uncertain interest.

- **Number of attendees:** How many individuals are attending the discussion? Two or three representatives? Or, on the other hand, six or seven? The greater the number of representatives attending, the greater the interest their company has in your business.

  The number of company representatives can send a powerful message to Western companies regarding the level of interest on the part of an Asian company. By way of example, the greatest number of individuals representing an Asian firm in a discussion that I have experienced with clients is fourteen. That included the company CEO, senior executives, the heads of all the departments that would be involved in the business, top salesmen, and the CEO's executive assistant. When the two executives of my U.S. client and I entered the meeting room and saw them all standing behind their chairs at the board room conference table, there was no doubt about the seriousness of their interest in our business.

Conversely, Western companies typically send fewer representatives—often one or two. While this makes sense from an efficiency standpoint, it is important to keep in mind the cultural significance that can be read into this in Asia. This is one instance where it is recommended to avoid being penny-wise and pound-foolish. The more important your business is, greater—not less—investment is advisable.

- **Number of departments:** The number of departments in the Asian company attending the discussion is another good indicator of level of interest. The greater the company's interest, the greater the number of departments that will want to participate. There are two reasons for this.

  First, pursuant to the Asian group decision-making discussed earlier, all departments that will be involved in a new business endeavor actively participate in deciding whether the company should embark on the new business project. To make informed decisions, they need to be involved beginning with the early discussions and negotiations.

Second, given that these various departments will be directly responsible for executing the business, they want to be as knowledgeable about it as possible, as early as possible in the process, so they can be best prepared.

Given these circumstances, the number of departments represented in discussions is a solid indicator of how serious an Asian company's interest is in your business.

- **Number and locations of major regional offices represented:** For example, in China are all the attendees from the nation's capital only? Or are the heads of the company's major regional locations present as well, such as Shanghai, Guangzhou, Chengdu, and Shenzhen. The same reasons for the number of departments apply to the number of major regional offices.

  In addition, attendees from major regional offices signal that the Asian company sees your business in their market as being nationwide, not limited to a few major cities. Beyond interest, it also suggests the ability to engage in your business on a nationwide basis. Such major regional offices in Japan would include Osaka, Nagoya, Shizuoka, and Fukuoka. In Korea, they are Pusan and Daegu.

I strongly recommend Western executives inquire during early discussions how the prospective Asian partner's way of engaging in your business might vary between the capital city and other regional areas. The differences can be significant. Sometimes differences are warranted due to the differing business circumstances in various parts of their country. Those do not generally represent a concern for a foreign company. However, I have often found that the execution of a client's business varied in geographical areas for reasons that are problematic and Western executives need to be aware of this.

For example, while claiming in the negotiations to be able to provide you with full, nationwide coverage of their market, regional inconsistencies in execution of your business can reveal that their actual presence and ability in those geographic locations is weak. You may wish to remove that company from further consideration as a result.

Another circumstance I have come across is that while an Asian company may have a regional location outside the capital city, the location is not appropriate or beneficial for the specific needs of your business in that market—another factor Western firms would be wise to clarify early on in discussions.

- **Seating arrangement of attendees:** Unlike in the West, company representatives all sit together on the same side of the table in Asia. They typically sit in one of two formations in negotiating meetings. And the seating arrangement reveals to you the level of progress of your discussions.

The first seating order is hierarchical with the senior most executive seated in the middle on his company's side of the table and the others seated on either side of him in descending rank within the company, similar to the placement of the pieces in the game of chess. Those sitting at the ends of the table will be the lowest ranking members of the company. This hierarchical seating order means your discussions are proceeding smoothly.

The second order is the departmental seating arrangement with the senior executive sitting in the middle but the other representatives are sitting grouped by their departments. This seating arrangement means that they have questions or concerns that they need to clarify before moving forward. Therefore, expect them to raise questions or points to go over in greater detail. They may opt to discuss your replies among their departments right then and there to ensure accuracy of understanding and allow for immediate and additional follow-up questions or clarifications. While this dynamic may add to the length and degree of detail covered in the discussions, it is favorable because it demonstrates genuine and serious interest in your business.

B. FREQUENCY OF MEETINGS

The request for follow-up meetings is another indicator of Asian interest in your business, both when the request for the next meeting is made and how far in the future the follow-up meeting is requested. Two weeks between rounds of negotiating is a good rule of thumb to keep in mind. Barring a special circumstance or event, if an Asian company does not want to meet within two weeks of concluding a round of initial meetings that generally is a sign they have limited or uncertain interest.

> The request for follow-up meetings is another indicator of interest in your business.

Likewise, a request by the Asian company for a follow-up meeting during an on-going meeting is an indicator of stronger interest than if the request comes after a meeting has already concluded and you have returned to your headquarters.

C. LENGTH OF MEETINGS

In some international markets, the length of a meeting is indicative of the level of interest in what is being discussed. This is certainly true in Asia. When Asian executives meet with you for one or two hours, their interest level is still not strong; meeting for four or more hours in one day shows good interest. When an Asian company wants to meet with you for two full days or more, that is a sign of very serious interest in your business. By way of illustration, the longest meeting I have experienced in Asia during the initial period of getting to know each other is three-and-a-half days of back-to-back, all-day and evening meetings.

D. LEVEL OF COMPANY RESOURCES COMMITTED

Given the Asian penchant for taking a long-term view of business, the level of corporate resources they state in meetings that they will commit to your business over time is a solid indicator of how seriously they view your business and their role in it. This includes not only the size and scope of their marketing and sales plan and the attending budget but also the size of the sales team they would utilize, the number of locations throughout their market, whether they will market and sell the products just through their own company or utilize sub-distributors and partners, and, if applicable, the number of sales channels they will sell in.

IV. GIFT GIVING

Exchanging gifts has long been a part of doing business in Asia. Doing so is not only a means to build good will as in the West but is also an expression of gratitude for the opportunity to work together. Gifts are a token of appreciation for the mutual business opportunity and relationship.

Foreigners are often confused about the gift giving protocol, particularly how often and on what occasions gifts should be exchanged. For example, do they have to be exchanged at every meeting? If not, when?

Commonly, gifts are exchanged at the initial meeting that takes place in Asia as well as the first that occurs in your market or other location outside Asia. I always recommend a third gift exchange on the occasion of the signing of the mutual business agreement. Once engaged in business together, gifts are typically no longer exchanged at a set frequency, but rather periodically. For example, gifts might be exchanged during meetings to celebrate achieving major milestones in the business project. It is also recommended that Western firms send their Asian partners greeting cards at the start of every calendar year for New Year's.

As you might expect, there are things to consider when choosing a gift to present. Here are two basic categories of gifts that work well.

Consider gifting an item specific and emblematic to your company. For example, one of your products either mounted or in a case, if they are of appropriate scale and make for a good gift. A jet engine obviously would not work, but a semiconductor chip in a display case would. Being encased in a display case is necessary if your product is a part and not a finished product. Presentation is important. In the event your company produces perishable products, a small replica of your product would be an appropriate gift. Another option would be a high-end item that has your company name or corporate logo or both on it.

Items unrelated to your firm or business are in the second category. These can include both high- and lower-end products. An example of a high-end gift would be a crystal vase, while a lower-end product would be a basket of special jams and preserves produced in the state where your corporate headquarters is located. One of my favorite gifts to present is a Mont Blanc pen. Highly appreciated by Asian executives, they are prestigious, yet not too expensive and, given their small size, easy to carry with you as you travel country to country and region to region around the world.

While in many Western nations it is popular to present a framed inspirational quote with an uplifting nature scene, an athlete conquering the heights of a mountain, or a crew navigating their sailboat in high waves during a race that can be hung on a wall, in Asia it is not common to decorate office walls to the extent done in the West. Except for the office of the company president, it is common to find a calendar and nothing more on office walls. So, such items would not be appropriate. Instead, small items that can be placed on a desk work well.

It is also advisable to avoid gifts that are size specific. For example, the letter-size paper we use in the States is not used in Asia. Instead, they use A4 size paper. Accordingly, a beautiful leather portfolio for an American 8½ by 11 inch note pad would not be an appropriate gift as their A4 size pad will not fit. It is well known how prevalent business cards are in conducting business in Asia, the significance of which is analyzed in chapter eight of this book. However, the size of business cards in Asia is different than in America—larger actually. Therefore, leather business card holders and cases are also not appropriate gift items. Since the countries of Asia use the metric system in measuring, not the U.S. system, avoiding size specific items is advisable.

It is advisable to avoid gifts that are size specific.

Additional items to avoid giving as gifts include:

- Letter opener, knives, or scissors – represent the severing of a relationship
- Handkerchiefs – symbolize farewell

- Umbrellas – thought to bring bad luck
- Cut flowers – used at the time of break ups

Other gift-giving considerations include the color and number of the items. While black is viewed as a sophisticated and elegant color in America, it is to be avoided at all costs in Asia as it is associated with funerals. In the same way, the number four is to be avoided in Asia as it is associated with death in those countries that use Chinese characters because the pronunciation of the words four and death are very similar.

Regarding quantity in gifts, it is noteworthy that in the U.S., a gift containing more than one piece such as crystal wine glasses or drink coasters is generally packaged with an even number of pieces—four, six, eight, or twelve. In Asia, gifts typically come with an odd number of items like three or five. So, while the gift an American executive might prepare will contain half a dozen pieces of one item, your Asian counterpart's gift to you is likely to contain five. No need to feel you were shortchanged by this cultural difference!

Finally, the common practice is for each company to present just one gift to the company they are meeting, regardless of how many individuals from each firm might be attending. This eliminates the worry about having enough gifts—it is one gift per company. It is also indicative of the fact that for them business relationships are built between the two companies more than between individuals—another example of Asia's group orientation.

The gift is presented to the senior representatives of the Asian and Western companies attending the meeting. It is common that the senior executive of the Asian company does not present his company's gift himself. Instead, a junior executive will present the gift. When small and medium-sized companies exchange gifts, the presidents or other highest-ranking executive may present the gifts themselves. It is advisable for international executives to follow the same protocol.

V. MEETING AGENDAS

In most Asian markets, agendas are highly recommended for all meetings and discussions, and they must be provided in advance of the meeting. Asians do not like surprises; being caught by surprise can result in losing face. Also, it would be rude if they were unable to reply to your query. They want to know in advance what will be discussed at the meeting, so they can properly prepare and avoid either party being embarrassed.

Westerners, however, may feel locked in by the pre-established meeting topics. To avoid this and allow for flexibility regarding the topics discussed in the meeting, I recommend always adding "Other" as the last topic on the agenda. This will help you maximize the value of the meeting.

In addition to an agenda, it is also a good business practice to send along a brief profile for each attendee on your team ahead of meetings. Adding an accompanying head shot is highly recommended. Providing these items in English is fine and is helpful and appreciated by the Asian company as it will assist them in understanding each attendee's name and role in your company. This is especially helpful for those Asians who do not speak English and would otherwise stumble through the initial introductions and name card exchanges with your team only to remain in the dark about with whom they are interacting. As you can imagine, that is not an ideal situation in markets where establishing a relationship has great significance, hierarchy must be honored, and showing proper respect is necessary.

Providing these three things in advance—the meeting agenda, brief profiles describing each person's role, and a head shot for each team member—goes a long way toward getting your meetings and prospective relationship off to a smooth and favorable start.

VI. NATIONWIDE SALES AND DISTRIBUTION

For the most part, companies in the West engage in business across their entire nation in a consistent manner. This is the result of our language, business practices, and other factors being relatively uniform. In the case of the U.S., for example, despite the fact that the country extends from one side of an entire continent to the other, firms can conduct business seamlessly in this geographical arena on a nationwide basis. This is not true in many Asian countries.

China and Japan, for example, are made up of dozens of provinces (or prefectures), autonomous regions, municipality areas, and special administrative regions. Within each country, there are multiple differences in regional languages, business practices, fragmented distribution systems, and the like. These variations often present challenges to foreign companies conducting business in those markets.

While nationwide marketing, distribution, and sales are, of course, present in Asia, they are not always achieved in the direct, straightforward manner or to the same extent they are in the West. Instead, marketing, distribution, and sales can be highly fragmented into regional and even local distribution networks. This may require putting in place a network of different regional or local companies to achieve nationwide sales. As a result, product marketing, distribution, and sales can require working with several sales companies and be more cumbersome, costly, and time consuming. These added layers contribute to the higher retail price-to-production cost ratio common for products in the region and bring with it the greater complexities and risks of a less efficient distribution network.

> Nationwide distribution in Asia is not always achieved in the straightforward manner it is in the West.

Efforts by U.S. and European firms to put in place nationwide sales and distribution is complicated—and often simply precluded—by the fact that the local sales and distribution systems operate based on decades old relationships that foreign companies do not have. It is not unusual in Asian markets for sales companies in their nation's capital to be unable to sell directly in local provinces since they lack the requisite relationships with local companies. They need to have developed ties with sub-distributors in those local areas to be able to have access to them, a situation that results in additional layers, complexity, and cost to sales and distribution channels.

Given its importance, Western companies need to fully discuss and clarify the sales and distribution capabilities of an

Asian company during initial business discussions, not later on. For major parts of the market outside of the capital region, it is advisable for Western executives to take the time to visit the sub-distributors that would be utilized there to handle your business and engage in appropriate firsthand due diligence. Foreign companies that neglect to do so can pay a terrible price down the road. On numerous occasions my consulting firm was retained by U.S. and European clients to get their business on track when this problem had resulted in market coverage that was problematic by being patchwork in nature and difficult to manage.

In the event an Asian company does not maintain a sufficient network of sub-distributors throughout their market, fragmented sales and distribution systems and the need for local business relationships may necessitate Western firms collaborating with more than one business partner in order to achieve full market penetration in an Asian country.

VII. REGIONAL AND HISTORICAL CONSIDERATIONS

In Korea, I was surprised to experience how small and medium-sized companies in Seoul and throughout the country often do not conduct business with firms in other parts of country. This is a remnant of the centuries' old rivalry and warfare between the three kingdoms that comprised Korea throughout most of its history (Shilla, Paekche, and Koryeo). As a result, engaging in business outside of one's geographic region and on a national scale requires a company to set up its own subsidiaries in different parts of the country. As this scaling is beyond the ability of many small and medium-sized firms, this regional dynamic is one of the factors that has contributed to Korea's four major conglomerates accounting for as much as eighty percent of the entire nation's economy today.

Western executives need to be aware of this history-based business condition and clarify during their early discussions with Korean companies their actual capabilities in providing comprehensive countrywide market coverage. This situation may necessitate adopting the alternative strategy of working with more than one business partner in order to build a nationwide business there.

Another historical consideration Western executives would benefit from keeping in mind is the language used when negotiating and conducting business in different Asian markets. Allow me to cite an example.

I was living in Seoul at the time and maintained an office for my management consulting firm in the Kangnam section of town. The vice president I had hired was a native Korean who spoke no English. I can speak only rudimentary Korean. However, he had worked in Osaka for six years and was a fluent speaker of Japanese. As that was the language we had in common, we communicated exclusively in Japanese. During a negotiation meeting with executives of a Seoul-based Korean company where none of the executives spoke English, I had the following experience.

We were seated on opposite sides of a long but narrow table. About five minutes into the meeting, the Korean company president sitting directly opposite me suddenly stood up, leaned toward me, and, grabbing my necktie, pulled me up so he and I were literally standing nose to nose over the table. He then began to yell at me in Korean.

While I could not understand what he was saying, the vehemence and anger behind his words needed no translation. Editing out the foul language, his message went along the following lines:

> *How DARE you speak that god-forsaken language in this country! Don't you know where you are? Don't you know the history between Korea and THAT country?*

This company president was articulating the ill will toward Japan that can be found in Korea even today, a consequence of the history between those two countries. It is important to know how the language that you and your translator speak can impact those you conduct business with in international markets around the world.

> It is important to know how the language that you and your translator speak can impact potential partners.

VIII. OTHER BUSINESS PRACTICE PROTOCOLS

DINING AND DRINKING

Sharing a meal as a means to build rapport is common in most countries, and Asia is no exception. Dining provides an opportunity to step outside of the formal atmosphere of business meetings and interact with your counterparts in a more relaxed and personal manner. It is an occasion to develop a greater familiarity and comfort level that contributes to and helps sustain the mutual business relationship of the parties involved.

The degree of importance and scale of dining, however, is not uniform throughout the region. Dining plays the greatest role in China where companies raise the typical business dinner to a new level and lavish complete banquets on foreign executives. Chinese companies often invite local dignitaries such as the town mayor to the banquets. This fanfare is done for the sake of relationship building and impressing foreign companies. It also helps to bolster their relationship and importance with local authorities. While dining is equally important throughout the region, it is not engaged in with the same fanfare common in China.

A key part of relationship building through business dining is drinking. It is seen as the opportunity for the members of both parties to engage and get to know each other on a personal level. This is especially true in China and Korea. As a customary saying in China explains:

> *The truth about oneself comes out when you drink.*
> *(jiu hou tu zhen yan* 酒后吐真言*)*

As is true in other aspects of business, propriety and ritual play a role in drinking in Asia where it is polite for the members of company A to pour the drinks of those in company B, and vice versa. But there are variations in drinking protocols throughout the region. In China and Korea you may pour your own drink but only last. In Japan, an individual never pours their own, unless they are at the bottom on the hierarchical totem pole in their company. In Korea, American businessmen and women need to be aware that drinking is often turned into a duel as Korean executives seek to see "what you are made of."

Over time I came to realize that these drinking contests

were not just to test my mettle. They were also an opportunity for everyone to de-stress and let off steam. While that may work for local executives who are accustomed to the practice, Western executives who travel to Asia need to keep in mind that this drinking experience on top of jet lag and the fatigue of the long journey can hamper their ability to be fully effective in business the next day. This is especially true if the Westerners are meeting with more than one company during the same trip to a country and have to deal with this night after night.

How can Western executives effectively deal with this business protocol? One method I discovered is to turn my glass upside down immediately upon sitting down for dinner and notifying my Asian counterparts that I am not able to drink for medical reasons. While they are visibly disappointed upon hearing that, it is understood and accepted.

IX. BUSINESS PRACTICES TO BE ON ALERT FOR

A. BRIBERY AND CORRUPTION

Bribery is illegal in most of Asia. While officially banned, however, Western executives need to be aware that it is nonetheless practiced to differing degrees throughout the region.

Outright prohibited in China, bribery nonetheless is part of conducting business there. The common understanding is that the government will look the other way when company executives engage in bribery but crack down on government officials who do. However, I can recount numerous times when I was expected to pay a bribe to government officials in order to advance client projects.

In one case, I was meeting with the head of one of China's government ministries to discuss the approval process of a client's products so they could be imported and sold. After showing the minister the ingredient list (names only), I inquired if any of the ingredients were problematic in receiving government approval. He spoke for five minutes in reply but provided no indication, saying it could go either way. I asked the same question later in the conversation, only to get the same result. I repeated the same inquiry for a third time and likewise received only a non-committal answer. Baffled, after the meeting I asked my native Chinese associate who had accompanied me to the meeting and had translated for me what the reason was. He replied:

> *Robert, don't you understand? When a decision-maker in China gives a vague answer when in fact he knows the answer that means he expects you to give him money under the table.*

Corruption is likewise prevalent in Thailand, Vietnam, and Indonesia. In contrast, bribery is least common in Singapore in Asia. The following diagram depicts the various corruption rankings of the major economies in the region.

Figure 12: Prevalence of Corruption in Asian Business: 2020 World Corruption Rankings

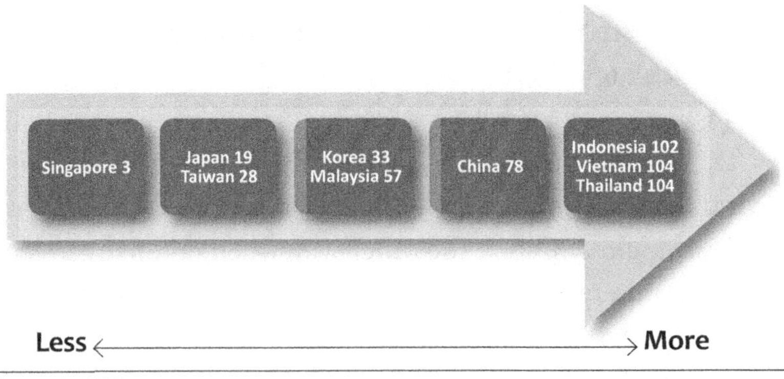

Source: Transparency.org, 2021

B. INACCURATE DOCUMENTS

Another practice Western companies need to be aware of in China is that documents provided by the company you are meeting with may not be the complete document, having information omitted so as to put a foreign company at a disadvantage. Another major problem and red flag is that the translation of documents may intentionally be inaccurate. As discussed in detail in chapter nine, it is imperative that Western executives have a native speaker on their team who can, among other things, verify the viability and accuracy of documents and agreements exchanged in international markets around the world.

Chapter 7

INTERNATIONAL MANAGEMENT CASE STUDIES: *Challenges, Failures, and Lessons Learned*

Even within one's own domestic market, unsuccessful business ventures are commonplace. In the U.S., for example, four out of five new businesses fail in their first five years, according to the U.S. Small Business Administration. Likewise, international businesses falling short of expectations or ending are not unusual. This is true for companies regardless of size and number of years of experience. This chapter explores the experiences in various Asian markets of both large multinational corporations as well as small and medium-sized enterprises with the aim to understand how Western company executives are challenged by Asia's divergent management practices and the lessons the reader can learn.

Looking at the case of Asia's largest market, we see that leading multinational enterprises have failed to meet corporate goals and ultimately exited in recent years. The following is a list of eight well-known companies among those that were unsuccessful in the Chinese market, along with the years of their operations there.

- Amazon 2004–2019
- Best Buy 2006–2012
- Ebay 2002–2006
- Google 2006–2010
- Home Depot 2006–2011
- Macy's 2015–2018
- Uber 2014–2016
- Yahoo! 2004–2015

In this chapter we will examine the varying management experiences of six companies as they expanded into Asian markets—two multinational corporations (Walmart and Amway) and four small and medium-sized former client companies of mine (PNQ, Inc., The A.M Corporation, The OTF Company, and GGD, Inc.).

I. WALMART IN CHINA – PITFALLS OF COOKIE CUTTER INTERNATIONALIZATION

Walmart was among the early group of multinational corporations to enter the Chinese market when it opened a store in 1996 in the city of Shenzhen. The company, however, was not able to achieve anything near the level of success there that it enjoys in the U.S. for numerous reasons.

The company's value proposition did not fit the needs of the market. Walmart excelled in the U.S. by successfully implementing its "everyday low prices" strategy through which it sold low cost, run-of-the-mill products to American consumers. However, as a leading, low-cost production country, the Chinese market was already saturated with inexpensive, generic products. In addition, Chinese consumers expected high-quality products from international companies. Also problematic was the fact that, while in the States the company sold packaged and frozen food products which are customary in the U.S. market, Chinese consumers prefer fresh food items. In short, both Walmart's product offering and pricing strategies were not suitable for the different preferences of China's consumers.

Walmart was not accustomed to the greater degree of government involvement in country's market. Walmart had to learn to navigate the political sector and the government's greater role in the economy in a way that it was not accustomed to for two reasons. First, as China's economy is a hybrid of a state-run economy and free market, the government plays a direct role in business. Second, as discussed throughout this book, it is not unusual for companies to interact with government to a greater degree than in the West due to the societal orientation of companies and the notion that government-business collaboration is natural. As a consequence, Walmart executives were required to deal with government officials in a direct and on-going fashion, which is in contrast to the West where legal and regulatory issues are delegated to corporate attorneys.

The role and reliability of the law was markedly different in China. Whereas the rule of law is indigenous and has been well-established in the West for centuries, it is a recent import from the West in Asia, including China. Prior to the impact of westernization, China's government and society had been based on the administrative bureaucracy and ethical precepts of Confucianism for centuries. This is true for all countries under Confucianism's influence. The affairs of state were actively run directly by government bureaucrats and based on ethical principles—not Western-style laws. As a result, China's current laws are often perceived not as rules that are written in stone as in the West but more as guidelines that officials throughout the country have flexibility in interpreting and applying.

Another problem for Walmart and other Western firms is that laws can be suddenly changed to their disadvantage. As we shall see in greater detail, this was also experienced in another case study in this chapter—Amway.

In Asian markets, the weaker role and reliability of Western law is especially prevalent in the early stages of adopting a Western style market economy. It is an example of the different "cultural soil" and indigenous building blocks discussed earlier that underpin management practices in the region.

Walmart's operating procedures were incongruous

with the market realities of China in its early years there. Not only was the rule of law weak but so were operating standards and procedures. The market was not ready for Walmart's precise operating standards and procedures, resulting in suppliers not being able to consistently perform at Walmart's intricate specifications.

The weaker physical infrastructure at the time Walmart entered the market resulted in the company not having access to the highly efficient supply chain its business model requires. Consequently, it took Walmart much longer to gain traction in the Chinese market. Not being able to gain a dominant market position prevented the company from commanding the type of bargaining power with suppliers that enables its everyday low prices strategy and success in America.

China's unequal geographic distribution of wealth and consumers has them concentrated in specific regions and the nation's largest cities (referred to as clustering). Rather than implementing a single, uniform national business strategy as it was accustomed to in the U.S., Walmart had to formulate and operate a multi-regional strategy, a much more cumbersome, involved, time-consuming, and costly approach. This greater degree of complexity is a fundamental aspect of international management, one that differentiates it from domestic management and challenges executives whenever they expand their company's business abroad.

The great cultural diversity of China's geographical regions results in greater diversity of consumer preferences than in many other countries. Walmart struggled to vary its product offering as its standard product line could not meet the more diverse needs of the market.

Aspects of Walmart's corporate culture and human resources practices were counterproductive in China. For example, the company's policy to hire a majority of employees as part-time workers ran counter to the collectivist values of Chinese society with the importance of workers being treated as valued members of the corporate group and companies providing employees with social aid such as long-term, stable employment. Incentivizing and training employees in the direct and individual-oriented methods of the West were not effective, a common difficulty in international human resource management as discussed earlier in part one of this book.

LESSONS FROM WALMART'S EXPERIENCE

- Companies cannot assume their value proposition and operating procedures that led to their success in their domestic market will be effective in international markets, a common negative result of the cookie cutter approach to international management. This is part of the luggage that executives should *not* take with them as they expand their business internationally, as discussed in chapter five.

- The societal orientation of companies and the notion that government-business collaboration is commonplace often require Western companies to work with governments to a greater degree in Asian markets.

- The degree of the rule of law in force in international markets has a tremendous effect on Western companies' operations and results. The weaker the rule of Western law is, the more indigenous the rules, practices, and values that govern business in a market will be. The result is management practices that are divergent from the international management practices that Western executives are accustomed to. In this way, the degree to which the rule of law is established is one of the major determinants of whether the management practices Western executives encounter in each international market are more indigenous or international, as discussed in chapter five.

- The degree of geographic distribution of infrastructure and wealth greatly impacts how straightforward attaining seamless nationwide distribution and sales is for a Western company as they enter markets abroad.

- The group-versus-individual orientation plus the greater societal orientation of Asian companies present challenges to traditional Western human resource practices. The result is diminished employee motivation, workforce stability, productivity, and bottom-line company performance.

- It is easy—and understandable—for companies to want to use the same management strategy and way of conducting business in international markets that their domestic business is based on; it is familiar and proven. However, this cookie cutter approach to international management and business development can significantly diminish company performance. Management is better served by taking the time to properly prepare for internationalizing their business, including customizing their strategy, approach, and methods to each unique market they enter.

II. AMWAY IN CHINA – REORGANIZING CORE BUSINESS MODEL AND OPERATIONS

Amway, the U.S.'s first major and largest direct marketing company, entered China in 1995. They were an early entrant into the Chinese market and their business achieved promising results during their first three years of operation. Then, abruptly, the Chinese government banned all direct marketing sales in that year. Suddenly, Amway and other direct sales companies such as Avon and Mary Kay had a major choice to make: write off their investment and exit the market or reorganize and execute an entirely new business model for that market. Amway chose the latter.

One of the requirements of the market that Amway's executives quickly discovered was the practice of businesses working directly with government officials. In this instance, Amway worked with the government as the latter drafted new legislation that would govern their industry in the country. While unexpected, this novel approach for Amway ended up providing several advantages to:

- Enable Amway to help shape the new laws in a way that would be as favorable as possible to their industry by better enabling government officials to correctly understand the realities of the direct sales industry.

- Better ensure that Amway—and the entire direct sales industry—would operate in China in a manner that is in the best interests of Chinese consumers and in line with the societal orientation commonplace among companies in Asia.

- Demonstrate to the government that the company was genuinely committed to the market for the long term.

- Show that it valued its relationship with its existing customer base and other stakeholders in the market by doing what was necessary to remain in the country.

The new laws required Amway to create and put in place an entirely new business model.

The new laws required Amway to create and put in place an entirely new business model. Usually, direct sales companies do not advertise or sell their products to the general public online or in stores. Instead, individuals register to become "independent distributors." Only such registered distributors can purchase products from the company; in turn, they sell them retail to their network of contacts. In addition, individual distributors sponsor other distributors and by doing so create their own downline distribution group. Like the company, individual distributors also are not allowed to advertise products. In terms of compensation, registered distributors receive a retail profit on their retail sales and also an override commission on the purchases of the members of their downline group.

In contrast to these traditional norms of the direct sales industry, China's new legislation required Amway to advertise, operate traditional retail stores, and sell products to the general public for the first time in the company's sixty-one-year history. In addition, the company's compensation plan also had to be totally redesigned along with the supporting data management and software programs supporting it. The company did succeed in putting in place a totally different business model and enjoyed strong revenue growth as a result.

Those fundamental changes, however, were not the end of Amway's need to reorganize its business model and operations in China. In 2005, seven years after banning direct sales, the government suddenly reversed itself again and passed legislation that now permitted direct marketing sales. After receiving its own license in 2006, Amway had to go through the process of reverting their business operations back to their original direct sales model. In effect, the company had to totally restructure and relaunch their business two times over the course of eleven years—a monumental and costly undertaking.

Was it worth it? Today, China is the company's largest market with over four billion dollars in annual sales and accounts for one-third of Amway's total global revenues.

LESSONS FROM AMWAY'S EXPERIENCE

Amway's experience in the Chinese market highlights the following management dynamics of conducting business in Asian markets explored throughout this book:

- Management needs to be patient in developing business in Asian markets.
- The requirement to plan, invest, and operate one's business with a long-term perspective is paramount.
- Management needs to be willing to be flexible to make

changes in the way the company structures, runs, and manages its business—including reorganizing its core business model.

- The company needs to be prepared to accept smaller profit in the short term for the sake of stable revenues and market share over the long term.

- Top company executives must be prepared to work directly with government officials on an on-going basis, as opposed to a corporation's legal department performing these tasks. Industry's relationship with government is not adversarial nor is it collusion but rather is collaborative and focused on what is in the best interests of society, a function of the holistic viewpoint of indigenous Asian management practices.

- Companies must meet the expectation to manage their business with a societal orientation that takes into consideration all their stakeholders and society at large, not just the company's own bottom line—the Asian version of being a good corporate citizen.

These market dynamics further illustrate the collectivist business culture and holistic logic of Asian management and markets. There is much to be learned from the lessons gained from understanding circumstances that large, multinational Western companies have encountered in their efforts to establish their businesses in Asia.

Next are four firsthand case studies based on experiences I had in managing business operations in the Asian region on behalf of my clients.

III. PNQ, INC.: WHEN SUCCESS IS DETRIMENTAL

PNQ, Inc. is the leading manufacturer of topical medical skin care products in the United States. This Beverly Hills-based company has dominated this product category for the past thirty plus years. Their brand is likewise recognized as a leader in its product category throughout the world. The corporation retained me as their consultant to assist with developing and managing their business in China, Japan, Korea, and Taiwan.

Given the prestige and popularity of PNQ's products and their inventor, both have been in very high demand in markets all around the globe for many years. Heightened popularity and demand such as PNQ was experiencing usually become the drivers for exceptional sales and market domination, and are, therefore, every manufacturer's dream come true. This was the case for PNQ in every other region around the world, but not in Asia where this situation created a nightmare. This was especially true in Japan, the world's largest skin care market then with an average per capita spending on topical skin care products four times greater than that of the U.S.

PNQ was approached by a mid-tier local pharmaceutical company about setting up a joint venture in Japan to import and sell PNQ's products there. As a pharmaceutical company, the Suzuki Corporation had all the requisite licenses and qualifications required for such a joint venture, since the products needed to be sold by physicians in hospitals and clinics via prescription rather than in regular retail sales channels because the product contained ingredients categorized as drugs.

Having a fifty-year history, Suzuki presented to PNQ's

management that it was well-experienced in selling topical skin care products in Japan's medical channel and proposed that the two corporations establish a joint venture. After each company invested $47 million in this joint venture, Suzuki then put their business plan in motion and sought regulatory approval from the Japanese government to import and sell PNQ product. It quickly became clear, however, that a main active ingredient in the PNQ line was not approved for importation or sale in Japan. This was an utter disaster for both PNQ and the Suzuki Corporation and their combined $94 million joint venture investment.

Suzuki took action to avoid that situation and recover its $47 million investment. By that point, Suzuki had received from PNQ all the details of the formulations for PNQ's products. Within a few weeks of discovering that the main ingredient was not allowed in Japan, Suzuki executives shocked PNQ by telling them that Suzuki was well on the way in developing a non-prescription, over-the-counter version of PNQ's product line that it would produce and sell in Japan. As it contained no drug ingredients, it was easily approved as a cosmetic product for sale and could be sold in various retail sales channels. Suzuki informed PNQ that in return for the rights to produce and sell this new retail channel PNQ brand product, Suzuki would pay PNQ a small percentage of the product sales as a royalty.

As if this situation was not problematic enough, there were several other detrimental circumstances that had developed around PNQ's products and brand name.

Given the high regard and great demand for PNQ's product throughout Asia, both patients and physicians in the region were eager to obtain and use the products years before PNQ decided to enter their countries. Aware of this untapped business opportunity, companies in Asia began to sell PNQ products in the region without authorization from PNQ. Among them was the TI Company.

The TI Company was selling hundreds of millions of dollars of product in the region through black market activity without PNQ's knowledge. Making matters worse, the PNQ products that the TI Company was illegally selling were knock-offs. They did not contain the superior ingredients that the bona fide products did, the ingredients that enabled the product line's exceptional clinical results and patient satisfaction. The result was that both physicians and consumers in the region became highly disappointed with the lack of results. This dealt a severe blow to PNQ's brand name *even before the company had entered those markets.*

PNQ's challenges did not end there. Skin care product users traveling abroad to countries where PNQ product was legally sold were carrying suitcases full of the product to sell to others back to their countries. These products were being sold by individuals who had no training in the correct usage protocols for these medical products. The result was numerous cases of disappointing results and cases of skin irritation and even skin damage from improper product usage.

In addition, numerous physicians in the region were claiming to have been personally trained by PNQ's founder and were, therefore, qualified to train other physicians as well as consumers how to use the product correctly. Given the very high-profile nature of PNQ's brand, these doctors could charge attendees thousands of dollars for each training. There turned out to be dozens of physicians throughout the region conducting these bogus training programs every month.

With all this activity, PNQ product was a big business in Asia. The problem was that none of it was PNQ's as they had not entered those markets yet.

In addition, all the unauthorized, illegal activity was hurting PNQ's brand name and corporate reputation. To make matters worse, Customs agents in Japan were intercepting huge volumes of PNQ product at airports and ports all over the country, none of which had received approval from the Japanese government to be imported or sold. News of these developments, especially the harm to consumers, became such a concern that government authorities were getting ready to officially ban PNQ products from the country. If that happened, PNQ would lose the opportunity to sell its products in the world's largest skin care market even before it had the opportunity to start its business there.

Put all together, these different developments resulted in significant confusion regarding PNQ's product and presented PNQ with a monumental challenge. It was at that juncture that PNQ retained me as their consultant. It would take the next twelve months to rectify these problems and allow PNQ to properly launch their business in the region.

LESSONS FROM PNQ, INC.'S EXPERIENCE

- Prioritizing regulatory status is paramount. Ascertaining the regulatory requirements for a product should be one of the first steps a company takes in preparing to enter any international market. This is not always the case, and companies pay a huge price as a result.

> Ascertaining the regulatory requirements for a product should be one of the first steps a company takes in preparing to enter any international market.

- Proactively working with government officials is a fundamental part of conducting business in Asia. To put an end to the unauthorized importation and sale of PNQ products in the region, I had the partner company I introduced to PNQ work directly with their regulatory and customs authorities to block and return all shipments.

- Conducting appropriate due diligence on potential business partners is critically important. The executives of PNQ, Inc. were shocked to discover that the Suzuki Corporation, a world-famous pharmaceutical company with subsidiaries around the world, had been working to formulate a knock off product line behind PNQ's back. Within Japan, however, it was common knowledge that Suzuki had a long-standing reputation for being a disreputable company that often did not honor its business agreements, especially with foreign companies. Failure to engage in proper due diligence prior to working with Suzuki cost PNQ twenty months of wasted time and effort, the loss of its $47 million investment in their joint venture, and significant additional remedial costs. Chapter five presents fifteen major criteria Western executives should use in screening potential partners in Asia. Chapter nine recommends another tool highly recommended for international companies seeking to conduct business in Asia.

IV. THE A.M. CORPORATION — IT'S ALL IN THE TIMING

The A.M. Corporation is a leader in the health and wellness industry. Through its groundbreaking research and products, it pioneered numerous new treatment modalities and products that for decades have benefited millions around the world, including patients at Harvard Medical School's Joslin Diabetes Center. When this U.S. company expanded its business abroad, it quickly achieved success in Europe and Latin America. In Asia, however, its efforts were less fruitful.

The company's first breakthrough product was a chocolate flavored meal replacement bar. Beyond just providing nutrition helpful in keeping up one's health and energy levels, its patented technologies and ingredients curbed hunger for four to five hours and helped stabilize blood sugar levels. However, unlike many other regions of the world, meal replacement bars were not commonly used in Asia when the A.M. Corporation launched in the region. Another challenge was that the only chocolate bars in the region at that time were candy bars. Local consumers did not perceive the company's product to be a health food, only as another chocolate candy.

From the perspective of international strategic management, A.M.'s product was too far ahead of the curve in the Asian market and, as a result, there was no demand for it. This is one of those ironic consequences of being the pioneer of a new product or technology. If it is too advanced and demand for it cannot be created, it does not sell well, and it does not become an industry disruptor. Effective market due diligence is essential.

It would take another decade before the notion of bars being medicinal or serving as a meal replacement would become accepted in Asia and a market for those products to develop. At that time, I introduced to the A.M. Corporation a Tokyo-based company that understood the product concept and its underlying science and was strongly committed to selling the product throughout the region—a true sales partner, not a distributor as differentiated in chapter five.

Our partner, the manufacturer and sales company RTJ, Inc., put in place a strong marketing plan for achieving its goal of multi-million-dollar sales in Japan in the first year of sales. It targeted several sales channels, including pharmacies, health food stores, TV shopping, direct marketing, and direct mail. Plus, RTJ exhibited the product at all the major, relevant trade shows. It allocated $2 million a month to promote the product and its underlying concept. At that time, the primary sales channel selling meal replacement bars was the pharmacy channel. To optimize the success of products sales in that priority channel, RTJ entered into a sales agreement with leading wholesale distribution company in the pharmacy industry in Japan, which gave it access to over ninety percent of all the pharmacies in the country, allowing for significant nationwide coverage. We were ready for significant product sales and market domination.

To jump-start sales of the product and at the same time

quickly get word out about the product, RTJ launched product sales through a major TV shopping campaign, a highly effective sales channel for new health care products in that market. From the very first installment on TV shopping, the product was well received, selling over a million dollars a day. Unfortunately, the success was short lived. And the cause was a failure of international management.

Japan has very high temperature and humidity conditions that have a great impact on so many categories of products sold there, including perishable food items. Chocolate products are susceptible to melting. Well aware of this condition, executives at RTJ raised this concern with the A.M. Corporation several times during the negotiating process. Given that their bar was chocolate covered, A.M. had anticipated melting as a potential problem even in America. Accordingly, they formulated the chocolate coating to include the very best anti-melting ingredients available in the States, and there had been no incidents of product melting domestically or in Europe or Latin America. Based on this ten-year track record on three continents, A.M. was confident that their bar was melt-proof and would be fine in Japan.

It quickly became clear, however, that was not the case. Not only did it melt, the contents leaked through the bar's foil wrapper. This was a highly problematic development and, as a result, sales of the product plummeted and A.M.'s reputation suffered a major blow.

To deal with product melting, executives of RTJ convinced the A.M. Corporation to allow the bar to be manufactured in Japan by the country's leading confectionery maker, the NT Company. Given the near one hundred years of experience NT enjoyed in successfully producing melt-proof chocolate products, this seemed to be a sensible solution. However, while NT's bars proved to be melt-proof, they could not produce the bars with the requisite moisture content of A.M.'s unique proprietary technology. As a result, the bars were too hard to be eaten and sales of those products also ceased.

LESSONS FROM THE A.M. CORPORATION'S EXPERIENCE

- A.M. Corporation's initial entry into the Asian market was unsuccessful due to differences in the culture-based customer preferences of its domestic and international markets. While American cultural sensibilities allowed consumers to be open to replacing a proper meal with a chocolate-flavored bar, consumer sensibilities in Asia did not at the time of initial entry into the market. While the notion of grabbing a meal or having a meal on the go was commonplace in the States, it was not in Asia at that time.

- Demand for a product exists when the timing of a product's entry into a country is in line with existing market trends or slightly ahead. If the product is so new, different, or advanced that product demand does not yet exist, generating demand for it is necessary for the product to sell well. International companies need to thoroughly research and ascertain the demand for their products in each foreign market prior to commencing business there. If their product is too far ahead of current demand, they must decide how to handle this challenging aspect of international management.

> Management's willingness to localize products does not guarantee successful international sales.

- The A.M. Corporation's experience is an example of the importance, and sometimes difficulty, of ensuring that products are appropriate for the conditions found in international markets around the world, in this case the challenge of temperature and humidity. While it is common for products to need to be altered to meet the conditions and requirements for different markets, it is important to remember that management's willingness to localize products does not guarantee successful international sales. As the founder and CEO of the A.M. Corporation remarked: "It's like trying to put a round peg in a square hole."

V. THE OTF COMPANY — MISCALCULATION, LOST OPPORTUNITY, AND THE GREAT PRICE PAID

The OTF Company is one of the top three direct sales companies in the U.S. While established many years after Amway, it quickly became an arch rival. International expansion was a major part of the company's growth strategy and Asia was the prize, accounting for well over fifty percent of the global multi-level marketing industry's total sales.

I consulted with the company as it prepared to launch in several Asian markets, starting with Japan. The company's sales estimate for their first year in that country was $25 million.

They had rented and prepared a corporate headquarters as well as a major warehouse and distribution center in a central location in Tokyo for their nationwide business based on that level of expected sales. Upon conducting my own market research, however, I calculated that their sales in the first year would be closer to $100 million than $25 million.

The company's actual sales ended up topping $125 million the first year. As the company had prepared its infrastructure in the country for sales of only one-fifth that amount ($25 million), preparations proved to be woefully inadequate. The company was overwhelmed by the scale and pace of sales activities from day one.

Distributors calling the company to place orders or for customer support had to wait on hold for two or three hours before getting through. Product, instead of being shipped within twenty-four hours of being paid for in accordance with the company's business model, took four or five days to ship. The size of the company's warehouse and inventory were insufficient and, consequently, core products were regularly out of stock.

As a result of these developments, the most successful network marketing distributors in Japan who had spent two to three years preparing for OTF's launch concluded that OTF was not a professional company and did not understand how to engage in business in their country. Most of these leaders of Japan's direct sales industry left OTF within the first two months of the company's opening, never to return.

Another development that caught OTF by surprise in the Asian region involved multiple distributor registrations. An individual signing up to become a distributor in one group and then subsequently registering to simultaneously become a distributor in another distributor group is one of the greatest headaches for multi-level marketing companies anywhere in the world. That type of multiple registration wreaks havoc on the stability and growth of the distributor groups and the company.

With nine years of business experience behind them at that time, OTF was accustomed to dealing with multiple registrations. However, the company never anticipated, and consequently was not prepared to deal with, the scale on which this occurred throughout Asia. In the West, distributors changing groups was not a common occurrence, and if they did, they would typically do so one time during their years of involvement with the company. In Asia, however, such change was rampant with distributors changing groups numerous times and in short order. Why did this unique situation occur in the region? The answer lies in the greater significance of relationships in the culture and business practices.

An existing distributor (distributor A) signs up another individual to become a distributor (distributor B). When B would subsequently be approached by another existing distributor (distributor C) with whom B had a closer relationship, B would simultaneously sign up in distributor C's group, even though this was against company policy. This would continue with distributor D, E, and so on. Relationship would obligate a distributor to feel he or she had to work with the distributor with whom they had the closer or more important relationship. This is another example of parties being *relationally obligated* to work together in Asian markets rather than *contractually obligated*, as discussed in chapter four.

The power and influence of relationships in Asia is the reason that multi-level marketing and the rest of the direct sales industry have always done well there and why the region has long dominated the global direct sales industry. However, because OTF was not aware of this fundamental, culture-based aspect of business there and did not adjust its management practices to take it into account, this trait became detrimental in the development of the company's business.

LESSONS FROM THE OTF COMPANY'S EXPERIENCE

- Appropriate launch preparations are essential. It is imperative that companies have as accurate an understanding as possible of the potential of their business in each target international market so they can prepare appropriately. In OTF's experience, ill preparation caused it to lose the best potential distributors in one of the world's largest markets for their product as well as great numbers of other potential distributors and retail customers who were put off by the company's shortcomings. Ineffective management practices resulted in the company not growing as fast or as large as it otherwise would have.

- The centrality of relationship in Asian business is one of the major themes of this book. Its importance permeates and impacts just about every facet of management in the region. OTF was not aware that parties are *relationally obligated* to work together in Asian markets in addition to *contractually obligated* as in the West and what that meant for its day-to-day operations. The result was that it wreaked havoc on its business.

Not understanding the role of relationships caused major disruptions and obstacles in the company's growth and stability. This is another example of how cultural-based differences in management fundamentals directly impact the speed and level of success firms achieve in international markets.

- If international executives invest the time to understand and prepare for the relevant differences in the management building blocks of foreign markets, instead of those differences hindering their performance, executives can get ahead of them and leverage them to advance their business interests. OTF failed to do so and paid a significant price. It is imperative for executives to examine how their customary management practices may need to be adjusted if they wish to achieve their potential in international markets. This is an essential facet of mastering divergent management practices in Asia and throughout the world. It is also why having an in-house facilitator interpreter is essential for achieving optimal success in international business, as covered in chapter nine.

VI. GGD, INC. — SNATCHING DEFEAT FROM THE JAWS OF SUCCESS

GGD, Inc. is an American company that pioneered and commercialized magnetized fluids. By successfully magnetizing fluids, the location and movement of those fluids can be precisely controlled. The GGD product came to be used in ninety percent of the world's audio speakers, half of the world's computer hard disc drives, and in numerous products in other categories. With tremendous sales success and market share domination throughout North America, Europe, Asia, and South America, they were the acknowledged global leader of that niche technology and product category.

The company already had a long history of doing business in Japan when they requested my assistance to help manage and improve their performance in that market. While their international operations were highly successful, that was not the case in Japan. This was especially surprising because so many of the audio speakers, computer hard drives, and semiconductors being produced in the world were being made in Japan. The Japanese market, consequently, should have been one of their top markets. However, it was not.

To deal with this situation, they hired a new director of international sales who claimed that he not only had years of business experience in that market but also was fluent in the Japanese language. They were quite optimistic that under his leadership their sales performance would improve significantly.

The new international sales director, John Allen, had already been employed with GGD for six months when I began working with the company. I was living in Japan and met him for the first time in Yokohama during his next visit to the country. We were meeting with executives of a Fortune 50 Japanese corporation that was interested in incorporating GGD components in its world-class products.

When meeting with Japanese executives together with Western clients, I always translate the discussions—English to Japanese and Japanese to English—in addition to facilitating the discussions and relationship building and providing strategic advice. However, as everyone at GGD and I had heard that John was fluent in Japanese, I did not translate as that meeting began. Right away I felt someone kicking my foot under the table. When I realized it was John and looked at him, he had a panicked S.O.S. look on his face. He signaled that he could not follow the discussion, from which time I translated for the rest of the meeting.

When the meeting concluded, John and I huddled to discuss it. When I asked why he needed me to translate the meeting, he replied that his Japanese was not good enough for discussing business matters. Keeping in mind that he had claimed to be fluent in Japanese, I asked him to clarify the level at which he was comfortable speaking the language. He replied, "To order sushi and beer in a restaurant." Knowing a few words and social greetings was the extent of his Japanese language ability. Needless to say, I was stunned. And so were GGD's executives back in the U.S. headquarters when they learned this.

The next day, John and I were to meet at the Tokyo headquarters of GGD's Japan subsidiary. It was my first visit to the company's subsidiary, and I had no idea of the surprises that awaited me there. The first thing I noticed was the telephone greeting for incoming calls. When several of the staff answered the telephone in Japanese, they did not say something customary as "GGD. How may I help you?" Instead, they answered with a different company name. This was puzzling. John and I attended several meetings that day with most of the discussion conducted in Japanese. I was flabbergasted when several quick exchanges were about matters unrelated to GGD's business. John had no reaction.

I decided not to approach John about this for two reasons. I had just learned the evening before that his Japanese language skills were minimal, so it was possible that he was not aware of these strange situations. And if he *did* know what was going on, then most likely he was a part of whatever it was. I decided to investigate quietly on my own. It was not long before I realized that in addition to engaging in GGD, Inc.'s work, the Tokyo subsidiary was also running a completely unrelated business.

This shadow business used all GGD's resources—the office space, staff, telephones, computers, printers, and copy machines. Even worse, as I was able to review more and more information regarding the company's income and spending, my suspicion was confirmed that GGD funds were being diverted to support this side business. When I made my initial report about this unusual situation in Tokyo to the Chairman of the company back in the States, he was incredulous. It was now clear why GGD Japan was not performing at the levels everyone expected in what should have been one of the company's biggest markets.

After I was able to fully investigate the situation, the Chairman instructed me to fire all those involved in the shadow business, assume day-to-day control of the company, hire new staff, and get the subsidiary back on track.

LESSONS FROM GGD, INC.'S EXPERIENCE

- For companies engaged in business in international markets, effective oversight is a critical component of managing internationally. This is important not only to prevent unwanted developments but also to ensure the company is meeting such fundamental goals abroad as:
    - Consistently proceeding in sync with the company's market strategy.
    - Operating in the most effective and efficient way possible to achieve corporate goals.
    - Advancing the corporate image and brand identity to the greatest degree possible and in the most desirable fashion.

Without effective management and oversight capability there is no way to know what is going on and, therefore, to successfully deal with the multiplicity of challenges Western businesses encounter in Asian markets on an on-going basis.

> Effective oversight is a critical component of managing internationally.

In the case of larger corporations, oversight is commonly conducted not only vertically through multiple layers of executives and managers in the international sales department but also horizontally through several departments, such as the organization's auditing and human resources departments. For example, larger corporations may have directors of sales for individual countries or regions where the company has business. This allows each country or region to receive a greater degree of oversight and management.

However, with small and medium-sized companies, often there is only one manager overseeing the entire international sales department. This means that one individual is responsible for all international markets. As a result, small and medium-sized companies generally have weaker oversight and management of overseas business operations than do larger corporations.

To be most effective, management and oversight must be conducted directly in the international markets themselves. No matter how effective the oversight and management function might be when conducted from the domestic headquarters, optimal success can only be attained with in-country, hands-on oversight and management. That is where the rubber meets the road and trying to manage international business operations from one's home market by remote control has severe limitations and numerous blind spots.

To achieve optimal oversight and management in Asian markets, those functions need to be conducted by someone who has, among others, the following three qualifications:

  - Familiarity with market conditions, business culture, rules, and regulations
  - Meaningful, successful, and recent experience in conducting business there
  - Sufficient proficiency in the language—speaking and even ideally reading and writing—to be able to engage in business in the language

- Reluctance to disclose the severity of problems creates the need for firsthand market information.

> Reluctance to disclose the severity of problems creates the need for firsthand market information.

It is important to note that when GGD's Chairman initially asked the president of the company's Asia subsidiary, Mr. Takahashi, what was causing their below-expectation sales results, Mr. Takahashi chose not to disclose all the facts of the situation, including that he was running a shadow business. He only acknowledged the full extent of the problem after I obtained the facts and they became known to the entire company. This is a clear example of the dynamic prevalent in business, government, and society at large throughout much of the region. Namely, reluctance to disclose the full extent of problems or unfavorable developments as discussed earlier in this book.

Why are negative situations dealt with this way? To avoid losing face. In recent years, the world witnessed this social dynamic in the initial handling of COVID-19 in China and the 2011 Fukushima nuclear reactor melt down and spill in Japan. In the business world, Western companies do not receive all the information regarding negative situations from their international partners and subsidiary staff, and, as a consequence, this dynamic presents a major challenge in managing business operations in Asia.

How can Western companies deal with this management dynamic? The solution is to maintain one's own direct source of market information and not rely solely on local business partners or government agencies in the region. This is necessary to:

- Better ensure you are properly and fully informed of what is going on.
- Be able to make decisions in the most-timely manner possible.
- Manage as effectively as possible.

- What are examples of direct market information sources Western firms can put in place?

    - Retaining on staff the company's own in-house market intelligence officer in international markets whose job it is to monitor news regarding unfavorable developments is one solution. In other words, a local market watch function within your company for the international market. To be effective, this market monitoring must be conducted on-site and in the local language.

- A second option is retaining a market research firm in a foreign market to specifically look for and report to you on developments likely to impact your business directly or indirectly, both in the near and long term.

- Verifying the proficiency of staff in the language and culture of international markets is essential.

  As GGD, Inc. experienced with its international sales director, even when a potential employee claims to be fluent in a foreign language, it is imperative that the company confirms the level of language ability and, equally important, cultural fluency.

  It is not uncommon in the U.S. for individuals to state they can "speak" a foreign language if they are able to exchange social pleasantries or carry on elementary social conversation. Unlike in Europe where it is common for people to grow up speaking three or four languages, most Americans do not speak multiple languages. When individuals become socially conversant in a foreign language, they are often considered to be able to speak it.

  The need to verify language ability is especially strong regarding Asian languages since they are significantly more difficult for Westerners to master compared to a romance language. An international executive managing in Asia knowing how to speak an Asian language is better than having no language facility. Being able to speak and read that language is even more desirable. As it can be difficult to find international executives who are skilled at both Asian market management and languages, a facilitator interpreter discussed in chapter nine is critically important.

As seen in the experience of the companies above, divergent management practices and the differing cultural norms that inform them are fundamental challenges to Western firms as they expand their business in Asia. Companies more effective in preparing for those differences prove to be more successful in their efforts than those that do not.

PART 3

INTERNATIONAL BUSINESS COMMUNICATION

The Stealth Determinant of Global Management

Chapter 8

THE LIFELINE OF INTERNATIONAL MANAGEMENT

"The single biggest problem in communication is the illusion that it has taken place."—**George Bernard Shaw**

"The most important thing in communication is hearing what isn't said."—**Dr. Peter F. Drucker**

International business is by definition intercultural business, and societies around the world embrace different views regarding the role, purpose, and expected dynamics of communication as well as management. Western societies, for instance, value direct, unambiguous, and straightforward communication. Comparatively speaking, Western languages require and can express only limited levels of respect. In Asia, societies maintain a fundamentally different view. Indirect, vague, and highly nuanced communication is the norm. Languages of the region require and are able to express multiple levels of respect.

The world's experience with COVID-19 provided a recent example that clearly demonstrates this difference in communication preferences. The Chinese government initially kept silent and then downplayed the severity of the pandemic to the world community for as long as it was possible to do. Western governments were appalled at this lack of open and direct communication. This was not the first time China engaged using this communication dynamic, however. Nor is it unique to that country. In fact, that communication dynamic is quite common in Asian nations. Japan's government did the same when the March 11, 2011 tsunami caused the nuclear power plant in Fukushima province to melt down and leak. China did the same thing with the H1N1 virus of 2009 and also with SARS in 2001.

What lies behind this Asian communication dynamic? The prominent 6th century BC Chinese philosopher Lao-Tsu—author of the *Tao Te Ching* which became the foundation of the philosophy Taoism that has dominated much of the region ever since—succinctly expressed this Asian view of communication as follows:

> *He who knows does not speak. He who speaks does not know.*

This is precisely what happened with the COVID-19 pandemic. The Chinese government clearly knew the reality of the disease but for as long as possible did not speak. In contrast,

Western governments which initially did not know the specifics of the virus spoke out. Both communications were consistent with Lao-Tsu's words.

Divergent views and functions of communication in Asia and the West are an ever-present stealth determinant in how successful companies are when they engage in business outside of their borders. What are some of the major divergent communication dynamics in these two regions? How do they impact management practices? What specific communication challenges do they present to Western firms in Asia? This chapter addresses this critically important facet of international management.

I. ROLE AND IMPACT OF COMMUNICATION IN INTERNATIONAL MANAGEMENT

Communication plays a critical role in business; indeed, it is the very lifeline of international management. It is the means through which every aspect of a business is relayed to, comprehended by, and executed by all stakeholders. Its presence, role, importance, and influence cannot be emphasized enough. Yet it is one of the most overlooked aspects of international management.

> Communication is the very lifeline of international management.

As Mr. Shaw's observation at the chapter opening illustrates, communication is not as effectively, completely, or easily achieved as is commonly assumed. This is true even when communicating within one's domestic market where there is a high degree of awareness and familiarity with one's own culture. When managing *internationally*, communication's import and impact are even greater. That is because when managing *interculturally*, communication is exponentially more significant, consequential, and challenging. This is true due to the divergent purpose, dynamics, and expectations that communication entails in each international market.

Let's get concrete. Specifically, how does communication impact management practices around the world?

- Communication is the vehicle through which every party involved in a firm's business exchanges information from business goals to implementation methods to placing and receiving orders to customer service. Ineffective communication results in ineffective information flow and bottom-line business performance.

- Proper communication enables accuracy in message content delivery, ensuring that what is conveyed is accurate and fully represents the intended message.

- Clear and effective communication is one of the major determinants of how successful companies are in obtaining their management objectives and bottom-line goals.

One of the most problematic areas in international management is the degree of accuracy of the communication between collaborating companies. In my experience in setting up and managing U.S. and European companies' businesses in Asian markets for four decades, communication accuracy between

Western executives and their Asian counterparts is approximately seventy to ninety percent. The result is a ten to thirty percent loss in communication and understanding.

When it was not my role to translate, I would nonetheless need to interject and either fill in the missing ten to thirty percent or outright correct the translation provided by interpreters. Insufficient accuracy or incorrectness occurs most alarmingly regarding strategies, objectives, expectations, and intentions of the parties engaged in managing businesses together across national and cultural borders. The loss in communication and accuracy occurs less regarding quantifiable information, such as numbers and tables. This problem is present in most facets and levels of a company's business; it also is commonplace in formal presentations at conferences, training programs, and trade shows.

This challenge presents itself in communications between international business partners from the initial negotiating process through jointly running businesses together. In the West, as we have discussed, we prefer communication to be direct and clear, succinct, and definitive. We prefer either yes or no answers; I agree or I disagree statements. In our culture, directness and clarity are viewed favorably to reduce miscommunication and to facilitate understanding, efficiency, and progress. Directness, clarity, and thoroughness add confidence that our communication will be effective and ensure that all parties are on the same page. Accordingly, a common three-fold rule of thumb in communication is to: (1) tell the other party what you are going to tell them, (2) tell them, and (3) then tell them what you just told them.

This communication dynamic, however, is not common around the world. By way of contrast, this is not the case in many

Asian, Latin American, and Middle Eastern markets. The result is that effective communication with international partners is highly problematic and is a major obstacle preventing companies from attaining maximum success. As a former European client expressed it: "Things continue to be extremely interesting. I really cannot put my finger on what the biggest problem we are having is other than communication with our new distributor in Thailand."

II. DIVERGENT GOALS IN COMMUNICATION

As is true in many international markets, the first challenge is that communication in Asia has a very different goal than in the West. In the latter, the purpose of communication is to express a thought as clearly as one can. We are encouraged to do so logically and convincingly. In fact, in describing a good communicator, we use such terms as easy to understand, clear, articulate, lucid, expressive, unambiguous, convincing, and compelling.

While the function of communication in Asia is likewise to convey a thought or sentiment, there is an additional underlying goal that is not present in the West that governs Asian communication dynamics—namely to promote relationship building and group solidarity. In consequence of having different goals and drivers, communication in Asia has very different dynamics and characteristics than what we are accustomed to in the U.S. and Europe.

In consequence of having different goals and drivers, communication in Asia has very different dynamics and characteristics.

For example, as was mentioned earlier, communication is intentionally vague in Asia, and people go to great lengths to avoid being too direct or clear when communicating. Statements that can be understood in more than one way are commonly used. Keeping communication vague means parties do not have to take sides by agreeing or disagreeing, thereby preserving and promoting smooth relationships and solidarity.

As a result of this common practice of keeping things vague, it is not unusual for business meetings to conclude with the parties wondering what just transpired and unsure as to where things stand. The experience of the Alamance Corporation discussed in chapter one is illustrative of this outcome.

When I initially experienced this practice of intentional vagueness in Japan in the early phase of my career, I thought the issue was that my Japanese language skills still had a long way to go. However, I quickly realized I was not the only one who could not figure out the meaning of what was said.

When I would ask Japanese colleagues, they replied that they also had no idea. The conversation was intentionally too vague to offer any clear understanding. When that happens, it is understood that a one-on-one follow-up meeting with the other party will be necessary outside of the official meeting to find out where things stand. Another option would be to enroll a mediator to assist. This could be because the other party does not agree with what was discussed or is not presently in a position to decide. If the other party subsequently does not agree to meet for such a follow up meeting, then it becomes clear that their vagueness was the means to indicate they are no longer interested in further discussions and their vague communication was simply the way to express disagreement indirectly.

I experienced this dynamic throughout Asia where it is more important to promote the favorable relationship between the companies engaged in business together than to lucidly provide the facts of the matter, present a solution, skillfully apply clear logic, or express one's thoughts convincingly or unambiguously. The gulf between these two fundamental communication dynamics is so significant that when Morita Akio, the co-founder and president of the Sony Corporation, was asked "So when you're in America you must be clear, and when you return to Japan you must be vague—is it hard to switch back and forth?" he replied, "It's more difficult than you can imagine."[23]

We have seen that with a primary objective of communication in Asia being to promote stable relationships, it is not appropriate to directly disagree, contradict, or challenge others. This is especially true when parties do not yet have a strong relationship, as is generally true when they are vetting potential foreign partners, negotiating, or in the early stages of conducting business together.

Most Westerners are not accustomed to this communication dynamic. For the most part, they do not even know it exists, illustrating communication's stealth presence in international business. As a result, while their Asian counterparts are seeking to express respect and promote a smooth relationship with them through vague communication or an absence of a definitive yes or no reply, Westerners typically misunderstand and interpret it as a lack of interest or believe that the other party is not being forthcoming. As Dr. Drucker stated: "The most important thing in communication is hearing what isn't said."

23 Accessed November 14, 2021. http://www.quoteswise.com/akio-morita-quotes-2.html.

III. DISAGREEING AND SAYING NO IN ASIAN MARKETS

If it is impolite to directly disagree, contradict, or say no to others in Asia, especially in formal settings or when the parties do not have a relationship, how then is disagreement communicated? There typically is a variety of means to do so, including an array of words or phrases that culturally convey "no" to the knowing hearer, even though their literal meaning has nothing to do with saying "no." In China, for example, it is customary to use alternative phrases and actions for expressing disagreement and saying "no." The following are examples:

- Use phrases such as:
  - *Hai xing/hai ke yi* – appears fairly passable
  - *Hai bu cuo* – seems not wrong
  - *Hai hao* – seems fairly all right
- Reply with a question
- Change the subject to another matter
- Become silent

As mentioned earlier, as a non-native speaker I am aware of more than twenty phrases used to offer a polite and culturally acceptable answer of no in the Japanese language. And that includes the word "yes."

While this same dynamic is common in Korea, executives in Korea interrupt and directly say no to a much greater degree than in China or Japan. In addition, they often say no more forcefully than their counterparts in the region.

This fundamental challenge of divergent communication dynamics is found not only in international management but also in relations between nations. The following is a true account of a state visit between the Japanese prime minister and the U.S. president where both the president, speaking in English, and the prime minister, speaking in Japanese, each reiterate their take on the White House meeting they had just completed. The president expressed his pleasure at the fruitful outcome of the meeting, noting that the prime minister had agreed to the U.S.'s requests.

The prime minister echoed him on the fruitfulness of the meeting. Regarding the requests the president asked of Japan, the prime minister stated that he will *zensho shimasu* (善処します)—correctly translated literally into English as "I will do my utmost best for that." Both parties are pleased with that message. However, the two parties actually made contradictory statements regarding the outcome. While the literal meaning of the English translation is that the U.S. and Japan are in agreement regarding the requests, the actual cultural meaning of the Japanese phrase *zensho shimasu* is "I do not consent."

> Divergent communication dynamics directly lead to misunderstanding and friction between the parties involved.

When Japan does not attempt to implement items discussed in the meeting, America concludes Japan was disingenuous. Japan, however, has a clean conscience because, according to their cultural norms, they not only clearly stated they could not agree, they did so very politely. This is a powerful illustration of how divergent communication dynamics directly lead to misunderstanding and friction between the parties involved—and this is at the highest level of government in the world's first and third largest economies!

How then can Western executives express disagreement without offending potential or current business partners? I have found two methods that work well to allow polite disagreement.

The response "That might be difficult" translates well culturally. You are not directly saying no, but you are indicating you are not in a position to agree. This response also suggests the possibility of a different answer in the future.

An effective second way to handle disagreement is to reply with a counterproposal. Verbally recognize their approach as one option, and then ask if XYZ would be another option. This allows you to come across as being open-minded and considerate of your partner's interests. A benefit to this approach is being able to offer a more desirable option for you that still could serve the interests of both parties.

The wording used in this option is very important. When Westerns offer a counterproposal, we typically phrase it: "*I have* an alternative option." By saying "*I have,*" the alternative becomes the idea of the person saying it—the Western executive. However, using the words "*Would another option be*" leaves the ownership of the idea up for grabs. Allowing the foreign executives to take your suggestion as a variation of their own makes it easier for them to accept it and later lobby for that idea within their company. It also demonstrates you are a partner concerned about the interests of both companies.

Asian languages readily facilitate this "would another option be" approach in discussions. In the case of the Japanese and Korean languages, for example, the counterproposal would have automatically been offered as "would another option be" since it is common for the subject of a sentence—in this case "I"—to be automatically omitted.

IV. LITERAL VS. CULTURAL MEANING

When I was working in a Japanese company early on in my career before I became a speaker of Japanese, I had an interesting experience that highlights another very challenging feature of many of the languages in international markets.

The president of the company I was working for at that time and I were waiting for the elevator. When the elevator door opened, an employee said to the president "*ohayou gozaimasu*" (おはようございます) as she got off the elevator. This means "good morning." The president replied, "*doumo*" (どうも) which, according to the dictionary, means "thanks." I knew enough of the language to understand what had been said and thought to myself that was rather an arrogant reply—the employee says "good morning" and the president says "thanks." As the company president and I were close friends, I felt comfortable asking him about that exchange. He laughed as he explained that while *doumo* literally means "thanks," it also is culturally understood to mean "the same to you."

The problem is that "thanks" is given as the meaning of *doumo* in the dictionary, but "the same to you" is not. As this example illustrates, an additional impediment in international business communication is that words and phrases often have cultural meanings in addition to or even different from their literal definitions that are not found in the dictionary. In this way, the actual cultural meaning of words and phrases sometimes has nothing to do with their literal meaning. This presents a significant obstacle to international executives managing in Asia who, unless they are fluent in both the language and culture of a market, are totally unaware of these cultural meanings.

It is well known that "yes" can mean "no." What is not as well known is that the word "no" can be part of the process of replying "yes." By way of explanation, if someone is offering something significant, it is not polite to immediately accept the offer. The more significant the item is, the more immodest it would be to accept it right away. Instead, it is polite to go through the protocol of saying "no, thank you" three times and then after the third time, to say "yes," thereby accepting what is offered in the end.

This interchange is similar to an American initially replying "no, thank you" to something being offered and then subsequently replying "yes" by saying "well, since you twisted my arm."

An additional challenge for companies managing across international markets is that this discrepancy between the literal definition and the actual cultural meaning applies not only to words but also to business actions and concepts. Examples include:

The discrepancy between the literal definition and the actual cultural meaning applies not only to words but also to business actions and concepts.

- The meaning of majority ownership. When France's Danone company and China's Wahaha Group formed a 51%-49% joint venture, the French executives understood majority ownership to mean that Danone would control how the company was run. However, Wahaha's management understood Danone's majority ownership to mean that while it owned the venture, Wahaha retained day-to-day operational control over the business and would run the company as they say fit. This divergent view of what majority ownership means was a major obstacle to their success and one of the causes of the dissolution of their joint venture.

- Offering an honorary position in a company or organization. In the West, we offer an honorary position to solidify the good working relationship between two parties or in recognition of assistance provided. In many Asian markets, offering an honorary position is a polite way of asking someone to become one of the major financial investors in the entity.

> The problem is not a problem of language, it is a problem of contextual understanding, expectation, and business application.

Thus, it is important for international managers to be aware that not only words but also business concepts and actions can possess different meanings, expectations, and implications. Because the problem lies in the contextual meaning of these actions and not their literal meaning in each international market, this problem is present even when Western executives manage or engage in dialogue with foreign partners **speaking the same language**, whether English or another common language. The problem is not a problem of language, it is a problem of contextual understanding, expectation, and business application. This dynamic is akin to the part of the proverbial iceberg beneath the surface that is unseen, unknown, and not understood—a stealth predeterminant of global management.

In this way, there are often two levels of reality in Asian communication. There is what appears to be the case given its literal meaning as well as what the reality of the situation actually is given its contextual (cultural) meaning. So prevalent and socially sanctioned is this facet of communication in Japan, for example, that the Japanese language has distinct words to clearly identify and express these two meanings and realities.

The first word is *tatemae* (建前). The meaning of these two characters is "constructed façade" and means what is ostensibly the case or meaning. It represents what is apparently the situation, or seemingly the meaning, or supposedly the case.

The second word is *honne* (本音). These two characters mean "actual sound." *Honne* means the actual situation or meaning. It is what is actually going on, the reality, what rings true.

In this way, the languages and cultures in international markets can go to great lengths to differentiate between what the apparent and actual situation and meaning are as a way to show proper respect, follow proper protocol, and maintain and promote smooth relationships.

In contrast, there is little tolerance for this type of communication in Western societies, especially in the U.S. The *tatemae* and *honne* dynamic would quickly alienate those you are interacting with.

V. SILENCE: ITS MEANING AND USES

Silence is another problematic communication dynamic in international management. In the West, it is not viewed favorably. It makes us feel uncomfortable and awkward, and we rush to fill it. In contrast, silence in Asian communication is often a pause to sift through and digest what is being discussed. It should not always be viewed negatively and certainly not as a problematic void that must be filled.

When communicating with international partners, how can one discern whether their executives are using silence to consider what is being discussed or if they are disagreeing? The answer lies in what they say after they break their silence. If their initial comment immediately after the silence is favorable about what was being discussed, then it is clear their silence was the opportunity to consider it. If what they say is negative or even just neutral, that is an indication of lack of interest or agreement. Likewise, if they break the silence by ignoring what you last stated and change the subject, that is a clear expression of non-agreement.

Knowing that Westerners are not comfortable with silence, Asian executives do occasionally use it as a tactic in business discussions to frustrate Western parties and trip them up. For example, they may use silence as a negotiating tool to win more favorable conditions. This negotiating dynamic is prevalent in

China, Korea, and most other Asian markets, but not as common in Japan.

How long can this silence last? Anywhere from a few seconds to a few minutes. The longest period of silence I have experienced lasted about two-and-a-half minutes. It can be a truly daunting experience as the entire room goes silent. What is the best way for international managers to deal with silence? Do not rush to fill it or ask if anything is wrong. Instead, maintain and respect the silence. Quietly sit and wait it out, perhaps by reviewing the points you have just made or will address next. Alternatively, enjoy a moment of reflection yourself. Doing so thwarts attempts to use silence as a discussion tactic.

It should also be noted that during the silence, it would be viewed as unprofessional and disrespectful to engage in an activity not related to the discussion at hand. For example, do not check for messages on your phone, boot up your computer, take out a newspaper, adjust your watch to local time, get coffee, leave the meeting to use the restroom, communicate with your company colleagues either verbally or in writing, or walk around the room.

VI. SIGNIFICANCE OF THE BUSINESS CARD RITUAL

Asian businessmen and women view and utilize business cards very differently from their Western counterparts. From their significance to the ritualized manner they are exchanged to the way they are handled, business cards take on a fundamentally different meaning and significance in the region. They play a powerful role in:

- Creating a connection between parties
- Initiating communication
- Allowing a relationship to commence
- Ascertaining the level of respect requisite of each party

What is the significance of the business card and the ritual of their exchange? The exchange of business cards signifies that a connection has been established. That has tremendous import in the regions where business is relationship based. After having properly exchanged business cards, it is possible and proper to begin communication with each other. Without having a connection, it is often not accepted to initiate contact with another party.

So inextricably linked are having a connection and communication that in the example of the Japanese language the word for "communication" also means "connection" (*renraku* 連絡). Because of this communication dynamic, cold calling does not work well in many Asian markets. One either needs to be introduced to the other party or to have the occasion to exchange business cards and establish a connection to then be able to commence communication with each other. Besides making it possible to contact another party, exchanging business cards socially obligates the other party to respond.

Simply receiving a card does not constitute a business card exchange. Each party must give his or her card and receive the other party's card in order for an exchange to occur. Given the power—and inherent obligation—of the business card exchange, it is quite common for executives in Asia to deliberately not carry their business cards with them as a way to avoid exchanging them and the need to communicate with those they may not wish to.

These executives, however, have their assistants carry their business cards. They are readily available for exchange, but only at the executive's discretion. When they are interested in exchanging business cards, they will instruct their subordinate to present their card to the subordinate of the other executive. This circuitous exchange of business cards is another demonstration of the indirect nature of communication in the region.

Another reason business cards carry such great significance in Asia is that they are a primary means for determining what level of respect parties need to demonstrate to each other. Asian societies are strictly hierarchical and both business and social etiquette dictate that the parties show proper levels of respect to each other according to their respective status. The business card is the only way an individual can know what their standing is relative to the person they are meeting, and based on that, what level of politeness is required. That is why business cards are intently studied in Asia the instant they are received—to determine the relative status of giver and receiver and by doing so ascertain the degree of respect each party is required to demonstrate.

The person in the lower hierarchical position needs to relate to individuals with a higher standing with a greater degree of respect. Conversely, the person with the higher standing need not express as great a degree of politeness to individuals with lower standing. Those different degrees of respect are expressed in two ways:

- Through the ceremonial bow
- Through the level of politeness in language used

Given the significant role that business cards have, they are treated with great respect in Asia. They are always presented and received with both hands—never just one hand. Never, ever slide a card across the table to the other party. Also, unlike in the West, it is not appropriate to write on a business card.

Asians generally keep business cards in a high-quality business card carrying case—generally made of leather. After business cards are exchanged in a meeting and the parties sit down at the table, they do not stack those cards or immediately place them in their pocket or attaché case. Instead, once seated, they will line up the business cards they received in front of them on the table corresponding to where those individuals are seated across the table.

In a final step of demonstrating respect, the business card received from the senior most person in the other party will be elevated by placing it on top of their business card case on the table. As the senior most executive is usually sitting at the middle of the table, his elevated card will be in the center of the row of business cards for those sitting on the other side of the table.

In Asia, business cards are viewed as a symbol of one's company, just as a flag is a symbol of one's country. This symbolism is another reason business cards are treated with great respect and why writing on them is considered inappropriate.

When engaging in business in international markets, bilingual business cards are highly advantageous as they allow the members of both parties to more easily verify the name and standing of each card holder in the other company. In markets with high relationship priority, business people are more comfortable interacting with foreigners who are on a similar level in their respective organization, so receiving a bilingual business card will also assist them in determining that status.

VII. COMMUNICATION DO'S AND DON'T'S

We have already noted it is not polite to directly disagree, contradict, or say no in many Asian cultures. When disagreements or conflicts do arise in markets with high relationship priority, it is expected that the principal parties will meet face-to-face and work out their differences in good faith. If they are not able to do this, they will utilize the assistance of a third party or parties. In the end, if the principals still are not able to resolve their conflict, it reflects negatively on *both* parties. The result is that both parties lose face in the eyes of society.

Chapter six discussed what venue and dynamics are appropriate as well as how to counter-propose and how to communicate "no." Other communication items to avoid when communicating with foreign executives include the following:

- **Humor:** What is humorous in one culture is often not so in another. Furthermore, it is difficult to understand and often misinterpreted.

  While it is common in the West to start a presentation or meeting with a joke or quick story to break the ice and help everyone relax and feel comfortable, this practice is not typically used in Asian markets. Avoiding humor in formal business discussions is a good policy, especially in the early stages of a business relationship.

In Asian markets, laughter can mean disapproval or embarrassment.

- **Laughter:** While it signals amusement in most societies around the world, in Asian markets it can also mean hesitation, awkwardness, disapproval, or embarrassment. When international executives hear laughter regarding something that is not funny, it generally signifies one or more of these additional meanings. It is advisable to take a moment to deal with this non-verbal cue of discomfort in your Asian counterparts.

- **Slang:** This is difficult to understand and translate correctly.

- **Double negatives:** They are confusing and difficult to translate. For instance, constructs like "We wouldn't disagree with your strategy" or "I can't not agree with your proposal" are difficult to translate. If the translator is skilled enough to be able to figure out the meaning of such double negative sentences, the amount of time needed to do so is time not following the subsequent conversation. The result is that you will lose part of the translation of what is being said. Either way, the use of double negatives impedes complete and accurate understanding of what was being communicated.

- **Idioms:** Idioms are typically misunderstood and, therefore, translated incorrectly. As a result, they can cause significant confusion in business discussions and management. As you can imagine, the following

American idiom examples translated literally into other languages would be as perplexing as they are problematic:

- "We had to cancel our outdoor marketing event because it was *raining cats and dogs*."
- "My company's CEO was so upset with my counterproposal that I was *thrown under a bus*."
- "There is more than one way to *skin that cat*."

On multiple occasions I witnessed the "I was thrown under a bus" idiom being used. In one instance, after it was translated literally by the Asian company's translator, all their executives were shocked to hear that my client had been thrown under a bus.

During a subsequent coffee break, two of their senior executives pulled me aside to ask me about the international sales director having been "thrown under a bus." One asked if the American CEO was truly that much of a madman, that crazy. He said he was not sure his company would want to do business with that company. The second executive said, "On the other hand, if their sales director survived being run over by a bus, perhaps we *should* work with their company. Who knows what miracles he might be able to perform to help our business."

- **Sarcasm:** This is difficult to understand and interpret. The result is that it is usually mistranslated, causing confusion or misunderstanding.

- **Long and compound sentences:** The longer the sentence you use, the more difficult it is to be understood and translated appropriately. There is a direct inverse correlation between length of the sentence and the accuracy and completeness of translation. The longer the sentence, the more unlikely it is to be translated both fully and accurately.

- **Speaking in long intervals:** Just as using long sentences increases the likelihood of weak and inaccurate translation, speaking in long stretches is a constant obstacle to complete and accurate communication.

  For example, speaking for two or three minutes and then pausing for translation is a much higher hurdle for the interpreter than stopping after twenty or thirty seconds to allow for translation. When making very important points, it is better to break up key sentences into parts to allow for full and accurate translation, part by part, than to risk an inferior or incomplete translation. Speaking in smaller snippets will increase the effectiveness of your communication and promote a more effective discussion.

  When confronted with a long statement by an international executive, translators who work for the other company are likely to ask you to repeat parts of it in an attempt to translate your entire thought. However, translators who are hired from outside translation services often do not. This is so for two reasons.

> Hired translators have no vested interest in the outcome of discussions.

First, unlike employees of the foreign firm, the hired translator has no vested interest in the outcome of the discussion. Second, they fear that asking for something to be repeated will result in the local firm that hired them giving them a poor evaluation when the translation service asks for its feedback. This problem is quite common in international markets and speaks to the inadvisability of utilizing outside translation services. The best solution I have found for this is the facilitator interpreter discussed in chapter nine.

- **Body language and hand gestures:** In Western countries, body language and hand gestures can play a significant part in communication. A frown, shaking your head, or rolling your eyes powerfully expresses that you are not interested or not in agreement. Hand gestures can be used to give added emphasis to a statement—such as pointing your index finger as you state your point. A thumbs-up or OK hand gesture can replace saying an entire sentence. While these forms of communication may be common in the West, in many international markets body language and hand gestures are not used or have different meanings.

- **Physical contact:** In many regions of the world, physical contact is not used when communicating. While younger or more internationally experienced

Asian business people will readily shake hands when meeting Western executives, they do not hug or kiss when greeting each other. They are usually greatly embarrassed by these gestures.

When Americans feel a connection with the other party, we may reach out and touch their forearm or hand while making a point or slap the other party on the back to express camaraderie or pleasure with a favorable conversation. This is not universal and should be avoided.

- **Eye Contact:** It is important to note that Asians commonly do not engage in eye contact to the degree that Westerners do. While in our culture it is rude *not* to maintain continuous eye contact when speaking with someone, the opposite is true in that region. It can be interpreted as impolite and even intrusive to maintain direct eye contact.

Due to these and other divergent communication dynamics simultaneously at play, the level of translation accuracy in international business is often lower than companies imagine. As noted previously, the average level of accurate and complete communication between Western and Asian companies ranges between seventy and ninety percent in my experience.

> Communicating in many international markets can be akin to working through a maze.

As a result of the significant differences in communication purpose, goals, and dynamics, communicating in many international markets can be akin to working through a maze. This is true not only for foreigners but even for native executives themselves due to the intentionally ambiguous communication practices.

Westerners going to international markets are often concerned about being polite enough and not insulting their potential business partners there. While this is certainly a valid concern, this and the next chapter illustrate that the challenges arising from different communication dynamics are significantly more fundamental and far reaching. They are ever-present in international management and act as a stealth determinant of international business operations and bottom-line results. The next chapter examines management tactics for successfully recognizing, dealing with, and leveraging divergent communication practices.

Chapter 9

ESSENTIAL ROLE OF THE FACILITATOR INTERPRETER: *Interpreting Beyond Language and Beyond Language Interpreting*

Translation is not a matter of words only: it is a matter of making intelligible a whole culture. —**Anthony Burgess**

The significance of the translator's role in international business is monumental. Despite that, however, it is often overlooked. This role should be a priority for any company that wants to maximize success and minimize risk in foreign markets. This chapter will further explain the intricacies and importance of the critical role of the interpreter in international management. It also will demonstrate how relying on a traditional translator is detrimental to a company's interests, both short term and long term, and explain why international firms need what I refer to as a facilitator interpreter on their team instead.

Despite its importance, it is common practice on the part of Western companies to give insufficient consideration to the translator's role or impact. I cannot count the times that preparing a translator for meetings with foreign companies was not even discussed by or placed on client companies' preparation checklists. Inevitably, they pay a tremendous price in terms of time, effort, expense, and results. In addition, they put themselves at a significant strategic and tactical disadvantage vis-à-vis foreign partners even before they depart their home offices for international markets if they do not have an appropriate facilitator interpreter on their team.

As English has become the international language of business over the past several decades, American companies take for granted that someone in the foreign company they meet with will speak English. Or if no one in the foreign firm speaks English, then the thinking goes that surely that company will arrange for a translator with the assumption that it is the responsibility of those who need help conducting business in English to arrange for a translator.

It is important to realize that the potential role and contribution of the interpreter goes well beyond translating the words of discussions and management's interactions with foreign partners. As this chapter explains, an appropriate interpreter is in a position to contribute to a firm's success in international management in several critically important ways including:

- Ensuring complete and accurate communication by providing the actual meaning and implication of what is being said.

- Advancing their company's strategic objectives.

- Facilitating appropriate relationship building and management.

> The role of interpreter should be central to any company's efforts to succeed abroad.

As a result, the role of interpreter should be central to any company's efforts to succeed abroad. There are several fundamental and far-reaching reasons for this. Let's explore them.

I. LOST IN CULTURAL TRANSLATION: THE NEED FOR CULTURAL FLUENCY AND INTERPRETATION

To be effective, a translator must be fluent in the language of one's own company and that of the international partner; equally important, the translator must be fluent and comfortable with the cultures of both countries. No matter how fluent translators may be in the two languages, they will never be able to convey fully and accurately what both sides are attempting to communicate if they are not also fluent in the cultures of each country. This is a major causal factor why the level of accuracy in international business communication only ranges between seventy and ninety percent as previously discussed.

We have seen in previous chapters the numerous ways

cultural understanding, or the lack of it, directly impacts managing international business operations. Without appropriate cultural understanding, a translator at best can only provide literal translations of what is being said. While literal translations may be correct "word for word" renditions, such translations often do not convey the entire meaning of the message, as discussed in the previous chapter. Literal translations often fail to capture the cultural connotations, nuances, implied meanings, and built-in but unspoken expectations—that is, *the actual meaning and implication*—of what is being said. A translator can only convey the cultural connotations and nuances of the speaker if the translator knows the connotations and nuances of both cultures equally well and understands the necessity of incorporating them into the translations and relationship building efforts.

In citing an example in the Japanese language, the phrase *kentou shimasu* (検討します) is a common response in replying to an idea or proposal that is presented. This phrase is invariably translated into English as: "That is worth our consideration." In an American cultural context, that is taken as a fairly favorable response.

However, as was discussed in the previous chapter when we looked at the example of the miscommunication caused between the U.S. president and the Japanese prime minister with a similarly innocuous phrase, the actual cultural meaning is, "We are not interested." When the translator provides the literal translation without conveying the culturally accurate meaning, the result can range from misunderstanding to complete breakdown in communication. Voltaire, the great French political philosopher of the eighteenth century, lamented the detrimental consequences of literal translations when he wrote:

> *Woe to the makers of literal translations, who by rendering every word weaken the meaning! It is indeed by so doing that we can say the letter kills and the spirit gives life.*

In addition to the difference between literal and cultural meanings, effective international business communication is hindered by the use of idioms, the need for indirect communication, the same business concepts and actions having different meanings, and other divergent communication dynamics found in the collectivist markets of Asia that were discussed earlier. These all speak to the impact of culture and the need for cultural fluency and interpretation on the part of the translator.

II. IMPORTANCE OF YOUR OWN IN-HOUSE INTERPRETER

How can Western executives know if their international partner company's translator understands the language and culture of both countries sufficiently to translate fully and accurately? The reality is that there is no opportunity to confirm the translator's level of understanding of one's home country language and culture when the Western executives have not previously met with the translator, and typically would not even have anyone on their team capable of confirming the level of understanding or accuracy of translation. Consequently, they are in the dark regarding how effective their communication is with Asian counterparts; Western firms are not only left in a precarious position but also are at a clear tactical disadvantage.

In addition, if a Western company relies on the Asian

company to provide a translator who ends up being their employee, that translator will act to facilitate the interests of the Asian company, not the interests of your company. The only way to avoid these handicaps is for Western firms to have their own facilitator interpreter on their team.

When communication is not effective with Asian counterparts, Western firms are left in a precarious position and at a tactical disadvantage.

III. FACILITATOR INTERPRETER: GOING BEYOND A TRANSLATOR

What is the difference between a traditional translator and a facilitator interpreter? A facilitator translator has experience in the business world and firsthand knowledge of what is being discussed, so they understand the context and the implications of what is being communicated. They are able to relay the contextual and strategic significance of what is being stated so the true intent of what the parties are trying to communicate can be relayed. In this way, a facilitator interpreter is able to ensure optimal understanding and advance the company's strategic interests.

The most desirable facilitator interpreter is effective in four distinct and critically important areas:

- **Correct linguistic translation:** Requiring thorough comprehension of both languages

- **Accurate and complete cultural interpretation:**

Providing the actual cultural meaning as well as unspoken implications and expectations of what is being communicated

- **Effective strategy development:** Helping ensure that discussions secure your corporate interests
- **Relationship building:** Ensuring that the level of respect, tone, protocol, content, and flow of the discussion are appropriate and aid in both establishing and strengthening the relationship with one's international partner

In order to fulfill this essential role, the facilitator interpreter must be:

- A member of your company's team—such as an employee or a consultant.
- Familiar with your company's business interests.
- Committed to achieving your firm's corporate objectives.
- Able to effectively speak about and promote your company's interests.
- Vested in the outcome of your company's interests and discussions.
- Fluent both linguistically and culturally in both your country and your foreign markets.
- Experienced in relationship building and management.

A traditional translator plays a two-dimensional role and can actually be an obstacle to achieving your company's goals for the reasons discussed above. On the other hand, a facilitator interpreter plays a three-dimensional role and is in a position to make major contributions to advancing your company's business success.

A traditional translator can actually be an obstacle to achieving your company's goals.

To express the difference between a translator and a facilitator interpreter, I use the analogy that a translator is comparable to a tollbooth clerk who collects tolls on a road while the facilitator interpreter is comparable to a traffic officer who directs the flow of traffic on that same road.

A tollbooth clerk has no knowledge of or interest in where your car has come from or where it is going. His only concern is to get your car get from one side of the tollbooth to the other. In the same way, traditional translators have no interest in where a Western company is coming from strategically or where the company wants the discussion to go; they simply want to get the discussions to go from the start of the meeting to its finish.

This is especially true for translators hired from translation agencies. They are satisfied with literal translations between companies. He or she is not concerned about how literal translations impact both parties, their business interests, or their relationship. Furthermore, the translator has no vested interest in how well the meeting goes or in the discussion's outcome. Finally, the translator has no interest in relationship building between the two companies.

In contrast, the traffic officer directs the flow of traffic to help you get where you need to go. When you put your left turn signal on, he knows where you want to go and will stop the oncoming traffic in the opposite direction so you can make that left turn. When you need to make a right turn, the traffic officer will stop pedestrian traffic so you can make that turn. In this way, the traffic officer knows your intentions and helps you move in the direction you want smoothly and with as little obstruction as possible. Likewise, the well-prepared facilitator interpreter will help a Western company achieve its corporate objectives by appropriately guiding the direction of the meeting, the flow of the discussion, and the relationship building between both companies.

Another example of the critical role of the facilitator interpreter can be seen when using the services of an attorney. When preparing an international business agreement, it is a matter of course that a company always has such an important document prepared by the attorney of the other company reviewed by their own in-house attorney to represent their firm and best secure and advance their strategic interests. That is standard operating procedure, and it would be foolish not to do so. In the same way, prudence dictates that when conducting international business Western companies likewise have on their team their own facilitator interpreter who is aware of, committed to, and able to secure their strategic interests.

By failing to take advantage of a facilitator interpreter's value, they unilaterally give up all the benefits the facilitator brings and place themselves at a significant disadvantage relative to their international counterparts who invariably have their own translator. And this disadvantage begins even before the first meeting or mutual business project commences. Companies will find that the cost of a facilitator is well worth the expense whether they hire a facilitator as an employee or contract with a facilitator as an outside consultant.

In many ways, the digital age and other technological advances have shrunk the world into a global village. Distance as well as time zones seemingly no longer keep people and markets around the world separated as they once did. Analytics and artificial intelligence purport to provide the common denominator for understanding the diverse people and markets around the world. While that may be true on one level, this book makes clear that on a deeper level the social and culture-based building blocks of management remain incongruous between the world's major regions. It is my hope that by utilizing the insights and strategies this book provides, companies and governments can better master Asia's divergent management practices and benefit from more insightful and successful international management.

APPENDICES

APPENDICES LIST

APPENDIX 1

Profile of Select Asian Markets

Item	China	Japan	Singapore	Korea	Taiwan	Thailand	Vietnam	Indonesia
Size (sq. miles)	3.6 mil	141,000	265	39,000	13,974	198,117	127,882	735,400
Population (mil)	1.4 bil	127	5	51	24	69	97	274
GDP* (US $)	14 tril	5 tril	100 bil	2 tril	586 bil	529 bil	261 bil	1 tril
Global GDP rank*	2	3	35	12	21	23	45	16
GDP per capita (PPP)*	20,984	46,827	105,689	46,452	57,214	21,361	8,677	11,646
State-owned enterprises	Yes	Yes	Yes	Yes	Yes	Yes	Yes	Yes
Type of government	Communist state	Parliamentary monarch	Parliamentary republic	Presidential republic	Presidential republic	Constitutional monarchy	Communist state	Presidential republic
Rule of law rank**	88	15	12	17	n.a.	71	85	59
Global rank for patent filings***	1	3	24	4	n.a.	38	51	43

SOURCE: *International Monetary Fund 2019
**World Justice Project 2020
***World Intellectual Property Organization 2019

APPENDIX 2

Building Blocks of Western and Indigenous Asian Management

Management Building Blocks	***The West***	***Asia-Pacific***
Purpose of company	Provide value to shareholders	Contribute to well-being of society
Goal of management	Maximize shareholder value	Maximize stakeholder value
Strategic objective	Short term profit	Stable, long term value creation and marketshare
Societal orientation	Weak	Strong
Scope of corporate social responsibility activities	Elective activity engaged in by choice to give back and enhance company brand	Fundamental raison d'etre expected by government and society, including contributing to national development and stable employment
Time horizon	Short term	Long term
Reasoning	Deductive	Inductive
Logic	Linear	Holistic/integrated
Outlook	Individual focused	Group oriented
Relational orientation	Independent and self-reliant	Interconnected and mutualy dependent
Importance of relationship	Low	High
Nature of business	Transaction driven	Relationship driven
Communication	Direct and clear	Indirect and vague
Purpose of discussion	Clarification of meaning and reach agreement	Gain understanding of context and implications
Meaning of agreement	Acceptance and commitment	Comprehension of meaning
Risk tolerance	High	Low
Decision making	Seniority based by position	Group based
(continued next page)		

Source: Robert Charles Azar, 2021

APPENDIX 2 (cont'd)

Building Blocks of Western and Indigenous Asian Management

Management Building Blocks	*The West*	*Asia-Pacific*
Company view of employees	Dispensable cost	Valuable asset
Employee view of company	Place to earn living, pursue individual career	Mini-society
Management-employee relationship	Neutral to adversarial	Paternalistic
Employee loyalty to company	Nonexistent to weak	Strong
Career advancement	Results driven	Seniority based also performance based
Human resource development	Focus on specialization	Develop broad-based company knowledge/skills
Importance of hierarchy	Low	High
Negotiation focus	Self interest	Mutual interest
Conflict resolution	Litigation	Good faith negotiation and mediation
Direct government influence on company decisions	Minimal to weak	Medium to high
Nation building obligation	Nonexistent	Strong
Cultural values underpinning management	Judeo-Christianity	Confucianism, Taoism, Buddhism, Shinto (Japan)
Economic values underpinning management	Hunting economy	Agrarian economy
Political values underpinning management	Laissez faire	Administrative state

Source: Robert Charles Azar, 2021

APPENDIX 3

ASIA'S HOLISTIC LOGIC AND MANAGEMENT

Holistic logic is at that the very core of indigenous Asian management practices. It serves as the foundation upon which business is conducted as well as the framework within which business has traditionally been conducted in the region.

What is holistic logic? What are its salient features and characteristics? What type of building block is it for Asia's indigenous management? What are its sources? This appendix addresses these questions.

Holistic logic is a comprehensive and integrative outlook that focuses on the entirety of a situation rather than on its individual aspects or components. Considering all things to be interconnected and mutually dependent, it incorporates an integrated perspective that takes into account the interests of all the parties involved or that will be affected. This worldview is based on the precepts and values of the traditional religions and philosophies of the region, namely Confucianism, Buddhism, Taoism, and in Japan also the Shinto religion.

Holistic logic places the interests of the group above those of the individual. For example, the interests of society are viewed as more important than those of an individual company. The greater good is prioritized over the interests of individual segments or components.

Relationships receive high priority in holistic logic and management. Accordingly, great effort is made to establish and maintain smooth and cooperative relationships. Business is conducted based on the foundation of relationship. Decision-making balances what is best for mutual relationship as well as bottom line performance. As a result, in indigenous Asian management, business is relationship-driven in contrast to the West where business is transaction or purpose-driven.

Holistic logic and management are characterized by a long-term perspective. They seek stable value creation and market share for the long term over shorter-term profit as is common in the West. It pursues consistent—even if smaller—revenue growth over multiyear periods rather than income that may spike in one quarter and be negative in the next.

Its preference for stability and steady growth can result in an aversion to risk and sudden change. Holistic logic typically gives priority to process over purpose—doing things in the established way (process) produces the best outcome. The result can be less emphasis on innovation (change) and more focus on improving existing processes. This dynamic is at the heart of continuous improvement (*kaizen*), just-in-time inventory, and just-in-time manufacturing that originated in Japan and have become global business best practices. The trade-off of giving priority to improving processes over purpose is the historically weaker presence of entrepreneurism in the region compared to the West.

Holistic logic impacts discussions. While it is common in the West for discussions to be organized so the topics are covered systematically in a straightforward and logical order one at a time, holistic logic results in topics being discussed in a manner that appears to Western executives to be disjointed and often haphazard—lacking what Westerners consider to be a rational order.

Also, it is common to discuss general topics initially and individual items later, a consequence of holistic logic's comprehensive and integrated outlook that prioritized the entire situation over individual items at first.

Agreements are likewise different in holistic management. Agreement does not necessarily equate with acceptance and commitment in Asia. "Yes" means "I comprehend what you are saying" and does not necessarily indicate agreement, acceptance, and commitment as in the West. Due to holistic logic's long-term perspective, it is expected that changes will be required to previously agreed upon terms as business conditions inevitably change year to year over time. This underlies the common occurrence in Asia of companies wanting to change the terms agreed to in discussions or previously executed business agreements. Holistic management's emphasis on relationships and its resulting dynamic of decision-making factoring in the interests of relationship often requires greater degree of compromise and concessions in discussions and agreements in the region.

Holistic logic's integrative outlook that prioritizes the interests of society over those of an individual company results in management viewing a business as more than a vehicle to earn profit. It views a company as an integral part of society that contributes to the welfare of all its stakeholders, from society at large to the individual employee. Management looks after the needs of workers beyond their job function by providing social benefits such as long-term employment, discounted housing, discounted company cafeterias, company vacations, a pension, and enrollment in health, unemployment, and workers' accident insurance. Firms are bound by a greater degree of social obligations than in the West. Consequently, notions of corporate social responsibility are fundamentally different and often result in companies not having all the options Western companies have, such as laying off workers. This greater intersection between companies and society at large results in the often-paternalistic nature of Asia's indigenous management practices and companies playing the role of mini societies in the lives of employees.

These aspects of holistic logic inform and govern indigenous Asian management practices. They impact the day-to-day operations of companies and present fundamental and far-reaching challenges to Western companies. Achieving optimal results in the region will require international executives to understand how to successfully navigate them.

APPENDIX 4

HOLISTIC LOGIC AND MANAGEMENT IN IT INDUSTRY BUSINESS MODELS

Asia's approach to developing IT businesses provides a lucid example of how the region's holistic logic results in business models that take an integrative approach to business.

The IT industry is comprised of several areas, including search, social media, online sales, and payment services. Western IT giants have tended to view those industry sectors as separate and independent, each as its own individual area of specialization. Accordingly, their business models focus on dominating one or a small number of parts of the total IT industry. Hence, Google dominates in search, Facebook in social media, Amazon in online sales.

Management of Asia's IT corporations, in contrast, views the industry comprehensively and, based on that, operate with business models that aim at dominating numerous sectors *within the IT industry*. In addition, based on holistic logic's view that all things are interrelated, they seek to develop IT opportunities *outside of that industry* in a great number of diverse industries. As a result, China's Alibaba and JD giants, Singapore's Grab Holdings, Inc. and Sea Limited corporations, and India's Jio Infocomm Ltd. provide products ranging from food to insurance and services as diverse as digital banking, healthcare, game development, pedicures, and ride hailing.

The focus of Western IT firms on individual sectors of the industry and the focus of Asian companies on diverse facets of the industry as well as non-IT industries as all being part of a larger, interconnected whole is consistent with the linear and holistic types of logic used respectively in the two regions. The result is divergent approaches, goals, priorities, and practices in the IT industry the West and in Asia.

Figure 13: Holistic Logic and Management in IT Industry

Facet of Management	The West	The Asian Region
Management's view of industry segments	Stand alone Independent silos	Part of larger whole Interconnected
Focus of management	One or small number of major segments within IT industry	Multiple IT industry segments Numerous non-IT industries
Goal of management	Profit maximization in one or select few major IT industry segments	Capture market share in multiple segments within IT industry Capture market share in numerous non-IT industries
Business model examples of major corporations	Single industry sector focus: • Google – search • Facebook – social media • Amazon – online sales	Multiple sector and multiple industry focus: • China – Alibaba, JD • Singapore – Grab, Sea • India – Jio

Source: Robert Charles Azar, 2021

APPENDIX 5

INTERNATIONAL MANAGEMENT STAFFING OPTIONS AND STRATEGIES

When a company staffs its international business operations, there are three basic options regarding locations from which to source executives to manage in the operation:

- Send home-country nationals
- Hire local managers in the foreign market
- Recruit the most capable executives from anywhere in the world

How do these three options compare? What are their advantages and disadvantages?

1. HOME-COUNTRY STAFFING

Using executives from the company's domestic market to fill international management positions

ADVANTAGES:

- Maintains a unified corporate strategy and culture across all countries because managers all come from company headquarters
- Allows for the transfer of proprietary knowhow and core competencies to foreign operations most effectively and quickly
- Use when qualified managers are not available in international market

DISADVANTAGES:

- Home-country executives often are not familiar with foreign cultures, business practices, and business environments—
    - Requiring a long and steep learning curve that executives go through with varying degrees of success.
    - Often resulting in management decisions not appropriate for the international operation.
    - Typically leading to less-than-optimal company performance.

- Local market nationals have no career advancement opportunity
- Can cause weaker work motivation, lower productivity, reduced company results, and employee resentment
- High cost of stationing home-country executives abroad
    - Ex-pat salaries plus housing costs
    - Relocation costs to move executives and their families abroad and then back home

2. LOCAL STAFFING

Local country nationals in foreign markets are hired for key management positions

ADVANTAGES:

- Helps to reduce the problems from different local business environments, management practices, and culture

- Provides career advancement opportunities for local country executives, increasing motivation, and avoiding resentment
- Cuts out the high expat costs for home-country executives

DISADVANTAGES:

- Less effective oversight of foreign operations
- Can lead to rift between headquarters and international market executives as a result of different national loyaltics, social pressures, and cultural preferences
- Can result in divergent strategic priorities, goals, and business practices

It is noteworthy that some countries in Asia require positions to be filled by their citizens.

- Foreign workers can only work in those markets if there are no qualified local citizens to fill the position.
- Workers sent from headquarters can only work in country for a limited time and must train a local employee in the needed technology or skill.
- When trained local employees are not available, staff from headquarters can work in Vietnam for three years and must train a local employee to be their replacement.

3. GLOBAL STAFFING

Company employs executives located neither in their domestic market nor in the country where their international operation is located

STRENGTHS:

- Helps avoid potential rifts between headquarters and foreign operations
- Provides career advancement opportunities for local staff
- Corporation can prepare a cadre of internationally minded executives committed to headquarters that can be sent to any foreign market
- Cuts out the high relocation costs for home-country executives

WEAKNESSES:

- International executives need to go through learning curve about headquarters and each foreign market

Figure 14: Major International Staffing Options: Advantages and Disadvantages

Strengths and Weaknesses	Home Market Staffing	Local Market Staffing	Global Staffing
Access to qualified executives to run international operations	Yes	No	Yes
Maintains a unified "home market" corporate strategy and culture across all markets, avoiding rifts between home-country and international operations	Yes	No	Likely
Strengthens the smooth and effective transferring of proprietary knowhow and core competencies	Yes	No	Possibly
Tends to result in local market unfamiliarity and inability to achieve optimal success	Yes	No	Possibly
Reduced career advancement opportunities for local managers	Yes	No	Possibly
Incurs high cost for ex-pat executives	Yes	No	Possibly
Can cause resentment in foreign markets toward parent company	Yes	No	No
Prepares a cohort of internationally minded executives that can be sent to any foreign market	Possibly	Possibly	Yes

Source: Robert Charles Azar, 2021

APPENDIX 6

Six Market Determinants of International Management Practices:

Prevalence of international versus indigenous management practices

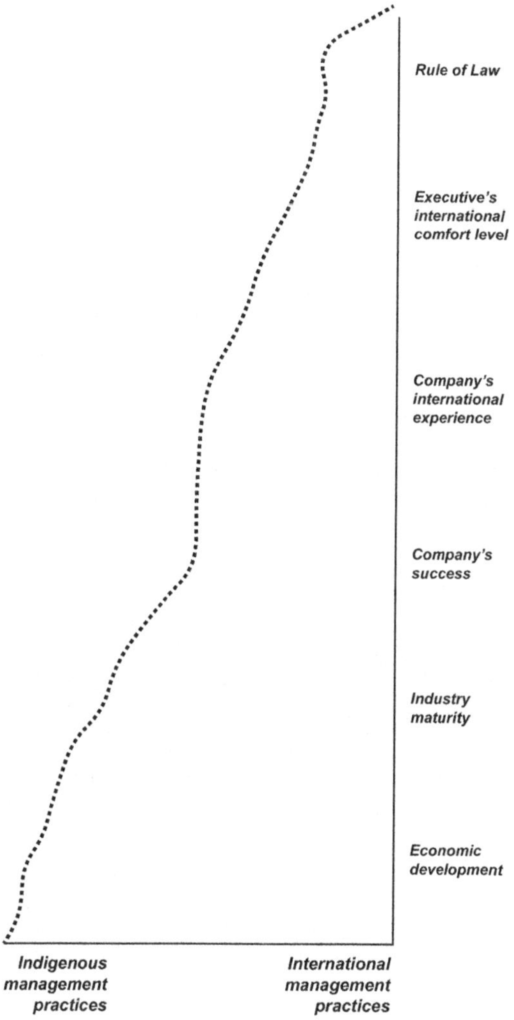

Source: Robert Charles Azar, 2021

BIBLIOGRAPHY

Anderman, Gunilla and Margaret Rogers. *Word, Text, Translation: Liber Amicorum for Peter Newmark*. Clevedon: Multilingual Matters Ltd, 1999, p. 124.

Aronson, Bruce and Joongi Kim, editors. *Corporate Governance in Asia: A Comparative Approach*. Cambridge, United Kingdom: Cambridge University Press, 2019.

Automotive News. "The DaimlerChrysler Merger: The culture clash heard 'round the world." May 6, 2018. Accessed May 21, 2021. http://www.autonews.com/article/20180507/FEATURE/180509923/the-culture-clash-heard-round-the-world.

Azar, Robert Charles. *Navigating Japan's Business Culture: A Practical Guide to Succeeding in the Japanese Market*. Raleigh, NC: WriteWay Publishing LLC, 2016.

Azar, Robert Charles. *Negotiating in Asia: A Practical Guide to Succeeding in International Negotiations*. Raleigh, NC: WriteWay Publishing LLC, 2018.

Chen, Min. *Asian Management Systems: Chinese, Japanese and Korean Styles of Business*. London: Routledge, 1995.

Cho, Fujio. Accessed May 22, 2021. https://www.azquotes.com/author/22307-Fujio_Cho.

Chokwatana, Boonsithi. "The Story of Thailand's Saha Group and its Chairman." Nikkei Asia. July 19, 2021. Accessed July 31, 2021. https://asia.nikkei.com/Spotlight/My-Personal-History/Boonsithi-Chokwatana/The-story-of-Thailand-s-Saha-Group-and-its-chairman-1.

CPP Investment Board. *Chinese Companies seek shift to longer-term strategies*. November 27, 2017. Accessed May 23, 2021. https://www.cppib.com/en/public-media/headlines/2017/chinese-companies-longer-term-strategies/.

Drucker, Peter F. Accessed May 17, 2021. https://www.goodreads.com/author/quotes/12008.Peter_F_Drucker.

Drucker, Peter F. "Managing Oneself" in Management. Accessed May 16, 2021. https://www.mbiconcepts.com/ibm-and-peter-f-drucker-first-article.html.

Drucker, Peter F. *The Essential Drucker*. New York: Harper Collins, 2001.

Fisher, Roger, William Ury and Bruce Patton. *Getting To YES: Negotiating Agreement Without Giving In*. New York: Penguin Books, 2011 third edition.

Forbes India. "Walmart's Passage to India." June 26, 2013. Accessed December 5, 2021. https://www.forbesindia.com/article/big-bet/walmarts-passage-to-india/6002/1.

Harvard Business Essentials. *Negotiating*. Cambridge, MA: Harvard Business Review Press, 2003.

Harvard Business Review. *HBR's 10 Must Reads on Managing Across Cultures*. Boston, MA: Harvard Business Review Press, 2016.

Harvard Business Review. *HBR's 10 Must Reads 2020: The Definitive Management Ideas of the Year from Harvard Business Review*. Boston, MA: Harvard Business Review Press, 2019.

Hino, Satoshi. Inside *The Mind of Toyota: Management Principles for Enduring Growth*. New York: Productivity Press, 2006.

Inamori, Kazuo. *A Compass to Fulfillment: Passion and Spirituality in Life and Business*. New York: McGraw Hill, 2010.

Inamori, Kazuo. *Amoeba Management*. Boca Raton, Florida: CRC Press, 2013.

Jackson, Keith and Miyuki Tomioka. *The Changing Face of Japanese Management*. London: Routledge, 2004.

Lee, Kuan Yew. The Finder. Accessed May 12, 2021. https://www.thefinder.com.sg/healthy-living/the-best-quotes-from-mr-lee-kuan-yew-for-business-leaders/?agallery=45025&aslide=8.

Liker, Jeffrey K. *The Toyota Way: 14 Management Principles from the World's Greatest Manufacturer*. New York: McGraw-Hill, 2004.

Loh, Boon Chye. "Taking a long-term view." The Business Times. July 28, 2019. Accessed May 16, 2021. https://www.businesstimes.com.sg/opinion/taking-a-long-term-view.

Lutz, Robert. Interview with Robert Lutz, Former Vice-Chairman, Chrysler Corp. Cited in Tuck School of Business at Dartmouth, The DaimlerChrysler Merger. Accessed May 1, 2021. https://docplayer.net/11234758-The-daimlerchrysler-merger.html.

McKinsey & Company. New perspectives on value and performance." February 2020. https://www.mckinsey.com/business-functions/sustainability/our-insights/the-esg-premium-new-perspectives-on-value-and-performance.

Min, Min, Mary Bambacas, and Ying Zho. Str*ategic Human Resource Management in China: A Multiple Perspective*. London: Routledge, 2017.

Morita, Akio. Accessed April 2, 2021. www.quoteswise.com/akio-morita-quotes-2.html.

Morita, Akio, *Made In Japa*n. New York: E.P. Dutton, 1986.

Ono, Sokyo. *Shinto: The Kami Way*. Rutland, Vermont: Charles E. Tuttle Company, 1979.

PHP Institute, Inc. *Konosuke Matsushita: His Life and Management Philosophy*. Tokyo: PHP Institute, Inc., 2002.

PHP Institute, Inc. *Matsushita Konosuke: His Life & Legacy*. Tokyo: PHP Institute, Inc., 1994.

QuotesWise: Soichiro Honda. http://www.quoteswise.com/soichiro-honda-quotes-3.html.

Rowley, Chris, Tae Won Sohn, and Johngseok Bae. Editors. *Managing Korean Business: Organization, Culture, Human Resources and Change*. London: Frank Crass & Co. Ltd., 2002.

Singapore National Library Board. *Singapore's Shared Values*. Accessed October 16, 2021. https://eresources.nlb.gov.sg/infopedia/articles/SIP_542_2004-12-18.html.

Sure Dividend: Warren Buffet. Accessed October 16, 2021. https://www.suredividend.com/warren-buffett-quotes/#management.

Taguchi, Yoshifumi. *The Managerial Ideas from the East*. Honolulu: Babel Press U.S.A., 2012.

Tai, Hung-chao, editor. *Confucianism and Economic Development*. Washington, DC: The Washington Institute for Values in Public Policy, 1989.

Tang, Jie and Anthony Ward. *The Changing Face of Chinese Management*. New York: Routledge, 2003.

Tian, Xiaowen. *Managing International Business in China*. Cambridge, UK: Cambridge University Press, 2016.

Tsukakoshi, Hiroshi. *Tree-Ring Management: Take the Long View and Grow Your Business Slowly*. Tokyo: Japan Publishing Industry Foundation for Culture, 2015.

U.S. Department of Labor's Bureau of Labor Statistics. Accessed May 8, 2021. https://www.edsurge.com/news/2017-07-20-how-many-times-will-people-change-jobs-the-myth-of-the-endlessly-job-hopping-millennial.

Varma, Arup and Pawan S. Budhwar. *Managing Human Resources in Asia-Pacific*. London: Routledge, 2014.

Wall Street Journal. "China's Coronavirus Response Toughens State Control and Weakens the Private Market." March 18, 2020. Accessed July 23, 2020. https://www.wsj.com/articles/chinas-coronavirus-response-toughens-state-control-and-weakens-the-private-market-11584540534.

Wall Street Journal. "Frustrations, Miscalculations: Inside the U.S.-China Trade Impasse." May 13, 2019.

Weiss, Jeff. *HBR Guide to Negotiating*. Cambridge, MA: Harvard Business Review Press, 2016.

World Economic Forum. *Explained, the role of China's state-owned companies*. May 7, 2019. Accessed March 18, 2021. https://www.weforum.org/agenda/2019/05/why-chinas-state-owned-companies-still-have-a-key-role-to-play/.

INDEX

ABOUT THE AUTHOR

Robert Azar is an international management executive with forty years of firsthand experience. He lived full-time and worked in the Far East for seven years, has an additional fifteen years of accumulated time residing and working in the region, worked in Asian corporations at the management level for ten years, and has developed and managed businesses in Asian markets for U.S. and European clients for thirty years.

Prior to commencing his career in international business and intercultural management, he completed a decade of formal academic training and field research in Asian politics, economics, and culture. His double major Bachelor of Arts in International Relations and East Asian Studies from New York University led to completing a Master's in East Asian Political, Economic, and Cultural Affairs at Columbia University. He then studied international marketing, global management, and business law at Harvard University. *Managing in Asia* is his fourth book. He also is the published author of numerous articles and reports on U.S.-Asian business, economics, foreign policy, and culture, published both in the U.S. and abroad.

As an expert on Asia, Mr. Azar has been interviewed often by major international media for more than thirty-five years. He has been a guest on CNN, CNBC, the Financial News Network (FNN), the Wall Street Journal Report as well as on local cable television and radio shows in the United States. In Japan, he has appeared, speaking in Japanese, on Television Tokyo's "World Business Satellite" (Japan's foremost business news program), NHK, Nippon Television, Fuji Television, and numerous radio shows. He has also been featured in several interviews in leading American and Asian news publications, including *The New York Times*, *BusinessWeek*, *Crain's BtoB*, and *Kenko Sangyo Shimbun* (Health Industry News).

Mr. Azar was honored to attend the White House's welcome ceremony for Japanese Prime Minister Shinzo Abe for U.S.-Japan trade discussions on April 28, 2015. He was also one of four hundred leaders in U.S.-Asian affairs to attend President Clinton's major policy speech before his summit meeting with then-Chinese President Jiang Zemin in Washington, D.C. on October 24, 1997.

Mr. Azar is one of only 10,000 consultants in the U.S. to have earned the Certifie-d Management Consultant (CMC) designation, the management consulting industry's preeminent recognition for demonstrated achievements and excellence in client satisfaction, professional standards, and ethical business practices.

His international career spans numerous industries and several fields of global business, including strategic planning, negotiating, management, finance, intercultural mediation, global business development, international sales and marketing, market research, international trade, product development, human resource management, trouble shooting, turn-around services, and political and economic analysis—in both the for-profit and the non-profit sectors.

Mr. Azar has logged over a million flight miles traveling to, from, and within Asia in service of clients. He reads, writes, and speaks Japanese fluently, is familiar with the Chinese and Korean languages, is a collector of Asian art, and paints Japanese calligraphy.

Mr. Azar has extensive experience in advising companies seeking to succeed in Asian markets. For further information, see *AsiaStrategicAdvisors.com*. He is often called upon to speak, present, and teach the intricacies of U.S.-Asian business and cultural matters to corporate, government, academic, and cultural entities. In addition, he is an adjunct professor of global business at the France-based SKEMA Business School.

He has served as a member of the board of directors for numerous organizations, including the World Trade Council, Institute of Management Consultants, American Cancer Society, the North Carolina Japan Center, United Arts Council of Wake County, and the Organization of Women in International Trade.

WHAT CLIENTS ARE SAYING

"With your assistance, we were able to increase our sales by 70% last year! A good percentage of our growth is attributed to your efforts in Asia. We anticipate, with your help, to continue to expand these markets and increase our sales even further."

— Marty Davidson, President & CEO
Excel Cosmeceuticals, Inc.
Bloomfield Hills, Minnesota, U.S.A.

"Koken Co., Ltd. has had the opportunity to work closely with Mr. Robert C. Azar over the past two years. We have found him to be an individual of utmost integrity and professionalism. Mr. Azar's knowledge of the Japanese health and skin care market is unsurpassed, even by our own executives.

"In addition to impeccable Japanese language skills, his ability to resolve difficulties encountered in doing business internationally is outstanding. It is without hesitation that I unconditionally recommend Robert Azar."

— Teruo Miyata, Ph.D., President & CEO
Koken Co., Ltd.
Tokyo, Japan

"These sales are really good news. Thanks for believing in us....You are a true hero! Congrats!"

— Arnd Kensy, President
& Ulrich Tobies, Director of International Sales
Human Med AG
Berlin, Germany

"I had the sincere pleasure of working with Robert Azar for many years at Obagi Medical. He was a life-saver.

"Robert assisted me in breaking into many Asian markets—Japan and Korea notably. His understanding of the physician channel, those companies/distributers who had the largest market-share in that channel and the key opinion leaders within those markets provided Obagi quick access and success.

"Robert's command on the Japanese language, his ability to understand the objectives of his clients, and his superior knowledge of the international market, make him one of the best all-round professionals that I have met in the industry to date. I would welcome, and look forward to, the opportunity of working with Robert again."

— Kathleen LaGrave, Former Director, International Sales
Obagi Medical Products, Inc.
Long Beach, California, U.S.A.

"Having worked with Robert Azar for over two-and-a-half years, I must say that he is very much involved in helping grow markets for American companies wishing to add sales outlets in Asia and Europe.

"Mr. Robert Azar is fluent in Japanese, which is very rare for an American, and I have found that to be an invaluable asset in promoting product sales in Japan. He also has very good contacts in Korea, China, and other parts of Asia, and excellent relationships with sub-distributors throughout the area. He has a vast knowledge of International Markets in general and a specific knowledge of various Asian cultures. And his focus on strategic sales is both unique and beneficial.

"I would definitely recommend Mr. Azar to anyone wanting to enter the International Market."

— William Kelly, Director of International Sales
Sciton Inc.
Palo Alto, California, U.S.A.

"I have known Robert Azar for several years now, and worked closely with him when he was engaged to provide services to Obagi Medical Products. Robert is highly skilled in launching brands globally and building an international presence.

"In one particular project, I worked with Robert to bring the Obagi brand to Japan. In the process of completing that project, it was very clear that Robert had extensive knowledge of the medical channels in Japan, who the key opinion leaders are, what companies had the largest market share, the best reputation and/or the highest growth rates, as well as who the best potential distribution partners would be for Obagi. Further, the key opinion leaders and industry players in Japan knew Robert, and it became clear that he has garnered excellent relationships throughout that country and many others.

"One of my existing contacts in Japan noted, after speaking with Robert, that he was very surprised that Robert was not Japanese - which is a testament to Robert's absolutely flawless command of the Japanese language and his natural understanding/competency with cultural norms and subtleties. Finding someone with these skills is rare - but adding those skills to his sharp business acumen and industry knowledge sets Robert even further apart. Top qualities: Great results, expert, high integrity.

"In short, Robert is a proven professional that delivered on all of the projects that we engaged him on and I would welcome the opportunity to work with Robert again, anywhere in the world."

— Curtis Cluff, Former CFO
Obagi Medical Products, Inc.
Long Beach, California, U.S.A.